VOYAGE *of* LOVE

AMY RENSHAW

VOYAGE *of* LOVE

'ABDU'L-BAHÁ IN NORTH AMERICA

BELLWOOD
PRESS®

WILMETTE, ILLINOIS

Bellwood Press, 1233 Central St., Evanston, IL 60201-0605
Copyright © 2010 by the National Spiritual Assembly of the Bahá'ís
of the United States
Printed in the United States of America on acid-free paper ∞

24   23   22   21   4   3   2

Library of Congress Cataloging-in-Publication Data

Renshaw, Amy.
  Voyage of love / written by Amy Renshaw.
     p. cm.
  Includes bibliographical references (p.   ).
  ISBN 978-0-87743-714-7 (pbk. : alk. paper) 1. 'Abdu'l-Bahá,
1844–1921—Travel—United States. 2. Bahai Faith—United
States—History—20th century. 3. United States—Description and
travel. I. Title.
  BP393.R46 2010
  297.9'3092—dc22
                                          2010028277

Cover design by Andrew Johnson
Book design by Patrick Falso

*Photograph of 'Abdu'l-Bahá taken in Dublin, New Hampshire reproduced with
permission of the Bahá'í International Community*

Author photo by Amethel Parel-Sewell

Contents

CONTENTS

Preface to the Centenary Edition

When 'Abdu'l-Bahá visited North America in 1912, our communities were grappling with challenges that still trouble us today. Among them is racial injustice, which has long deprived many individuals of true freedom. In the early 1900s, even more so than now, schools and neighborhoods across the United States were segregated by race. Opportunities for people of color were restricted by racist laws and policies or by deeply held prejudices.

But as the Son of Bahá'u'lláh, the Bahá'í Faith's Founder, 'Abdu'l-Bahá held a radically different view of racial diversity. He toured the land for eight months, warmly embracing people of all cultures and backgrounds. At times He compared diverse races to colorful flowers or sparkling jewels. At an integrated event in Washington, D.C., He joyfully exclaimed, "How beautiful to see blacks and whites together!" He confronted the assumptions of the time with a promising vision of oneness: "My hope is that the white and the black will be united in perfect love and fellowship, with complete unity and brotherhood."*

When 'Abdu'l-Bahá returned home to what is now Israel, He continued to send loving guidance to the West. In 1916 and 1917, as World War I raged, He wrote fourteen prayer-filled letters to the Bahá'ís of the United States and Canada. He had unshakable faith in our potential for peace-building, writing, "Exert yourselves; your mission is unspeakably glorious. Should success crown your enterprise, America will assuredly evolve into a center from which waves of spiritual power will emanate. . . ."*

Clearly, the path to this destiny is full of setbacks and challenges. Today, a century after the passing of 'Abdu'l-Bahá, the United States is still polluted by racism. Cross-racial friendships and vibrantly diverse neighborhoods and schools are far from commonplace. Systemic racism persists in housing, education, employment, policing—everywhere, in fact. Creating equity takes diligent, ongoing effort.

At this point in history, the global Bahá'í community pauses to reflect on the life of 'Abdu'l-Bahá, Who exemplified the Bahá'í teachings. He left this world in the early hours of November 28, 1921, in Haifa, Israel. Messages flew around the world, bringing condolences to His family from government officials and from broken-hearted Bahá'ís.

The next day, about 10,000 mourners gathered in the streets of Haifa to pay their respects. They included people from every walk of life. Men, women, and children followed His coffin up the slope of

---

* 'Abdu'l-Bahá, *The Promulgation of Universal Peace*, p. 602.
* 'Abdu'l-Bahá, *Tablets of the Divine Plan*, no. 11.

Mount Carmel. Muslim, Christian, and Jewish dignitaries gave speeches praising His kindness and wisdom. Newspapers around the globe published stories about Him. His earthly remains were laid to rest in a chamber of the Shrine of the Báb, the Prophet Herald of the Bahá'í Faith.

Just as 'Abdu'l-Bahá had served those in need during His lifetime, generosity poured out in His name. In the first week after His passing, hundreds of the poor were fed at His home. On the seventh day, corn was distributed to about a thousand people. On the fortieth day, a memorial feast was held for six hundred, including high-ranking officials, and a hundred of the poor were given sustenance.

A century has now passed since 'Abdu'l-Bahá walked on the Earth. Still, His words, actions, and devotion continue to guide millions of Bahá'ís and friends of the Bahá'í Faith. As we commemorate His life at this turning point, we can strive, as He did, to welcome all people with friendship and love.

In the stories and excerpts collected here, we meet some of the people whose lives were transformed by encountering 'Abdu'l-Bahá. We learn about their reactions to His inspiring words and all-encompassing love. And we can take action to right the wrongs He urged us to address so long ago.

In His Will and Testament, read publicly in January 1922, 'Abdu'l-Bahá gave us these marching orders:

It is incumbent upon everyone to show the utmost love, rectitude of conduct, straightforwardness and sincere kindliness unto all the peoples and kindreds of the world, be they friends or strangers. So intense must be the spirit of love and loving kindness, that the stranger may find himself a friend, the enemy a true brother, no difference whatsoever existing between them. . . . Consort with all the peoples, kindreds and religions of the world with the utmost truthfulness, uprightness, faithfulness, kindliness, good-will and friendliness, that all the world of being may be filled with the holy ecstasy of the grace of Bahá, that ignorance, enmity, hate and rancor may vanish from the world and the darkness of estrangement amidst the peoples and kindreds of the world may give way to the Light of Unity.*

February 2021

* 'Abdu'l-Bahá, *Will and Testament of 'Abdu'l-Bahá,* no. 1.23.

Note to the Reader

A wide variety of historical sources was used in this book to provide a broad overview of 'Abdu'l-Bahá's visit to North America, His interactions with the early Bahá'ís, and the social conditions of the time. Some of these sources consist of Bahá'ís' personal recollections of 'Abdu'l-Bahá and His statements to them. These accounts offer valuable insights into the early Bahá'í community and its members' relationships with 'Abdu'l-Bahá. However, they cannot be considered authentic sources of 'Abdu'l-Bahá's words. They should be used with caution, keeping in mind that they may include errors or misunderstandings on the part of the original authors. However, *Mahmúd's Diary*, recorded by 'Abdu'l-Bahá's companion Mahmúd-i-Zarqání, is considered an authentic record of 'Abdu'l-Bahá's words. Most of the quotations from 'Abdu'l-Bahá's public talks are from the book *The Promulgation of Universal Peace*, the publication of which He encouraged.

Introduction

Have you ever felt nervous about speaking in front of a large group of people? Have you ever been far away from home for a long time and felt homesick? Imagine traveling to a different country, thousands of miles from your home, and speaking to thousands of people at a time. Imagine that you speak a different language from your audience and wear clothing that looks strange to them. Now imagine talking to groups large and small almost every day, sometimes giving five speeches a day, for eight months. How would you feel?

'Abdu'l-Bahá did all of these things with tremendous energy and joy. As the eldest Son of Bahá'u'lláh, the Founder of the Bahá'í Faith, 'Abdu'l-Bahá had spent most of His life in exile and imprisonment. Like His Father, He was innocent of any crime. Officials persecuted Bahá'u'lláh, His family, and many of His followers in an effort to stop the growth of the Bahá'í Faith. Still, the new religion grew, and in time it reached North America.

'Abdu'l-Bahá came to the United States when He was nearly sixty-eight years old, just a few years after gaining His freedom from imprisonment in the city of 'Akká, located in what is now Israel. His health was poor, but He amazed everyone with His strength and vitality. For eight months, He traveled across the country and into Canada, speaking about the Bahá'í Faith at colleges, in churches, in private homes, and in many other places. He covered more than five thousand miles. He spoke privately with hundreds of individuals. Friends offered Him money for His expenses, but He refused to accept any gifts for Himself. Instead, He encouraged people to give to the poor.

In North America at that time, it was unusual to have visitors from the Middle East. Though the Bahá'í Faith was not widely known, 'Abdu'l-Bahá attracted a great deal of attention from newspapers. They called Him a "Persian Teacher of World Peace," "Head of Newest Religion," and "Famous Persian Religious Leader."[1]

Among the small group of North American Bahá'ís, the effect of 'Abdu'l-Bahá's visit was powerful. A few had been able to make the ocean voyage to see Him, but for most, the trip was too costly. His journey was their only chance to see the leader of their Faith, Who had been appointed by Bahá'u'lláh to interpret His writings and guide the Bahá'ís after His passing.

The reflections of many of the Bahá'ís upon seeing 'Abdu'l-Bahá convey their great admiration for Him. Many called Him "the Master," a term Bahá'u'lláh Himself had used for His Son. One writer described 'Abdu'l-Bahá's "humility, the never failing love,—but above all, the sense of power mingled with gentleness. . . ."[2] Another wrote of His "majesty combined with exquisite courtesy. . . . Such gentleness, such love emanated from Him as I had never seen."[3] One Bahá'í described His "flashing eyes" that seemed to pierce the soul.[4] Another wrote, "It seemed as though never before had anyone really seen *me*."[5]

His voice was described as "a resonant bell of finest timbre; never loud but of such penetrating quality that the walls of the room seemed to vibrate with its music."[6] 'Abdu'l-Bahá also had a lively sense of humor. A Bahá'í noted "His boyish hearty laughter" that "rang through the room. . . ."[7] And a companion wrote of one of His talks, "I will never forget the joy and excitement of the audience. . . . peals of laughter could be heard outside the building."[8]

Some people, including journalists, were confused about 'Abdu'l-Bahá's station and referred to Him as a "Prophet." But 'Abdu'l-Bahá always emphasized humility. Though His given name was 'Abbás, He chose for Himself the title of "'Abdu'l-Bahá," which means "Servant of Bahá."

'Abdu'l-Bahá came to the West to envelop the Bahá'ís in His loving embrace. He said that His friends in the East had urged Him not to make the difficult journey. They feared that His health could not bear the trip. But 'Abdu'l-Bahá said, "When it is necessary, my body can endure everything. It has withstood forty years of imprisonment and can still undergo the utmost trials." He told the Bahá'ís, "This long voyage will prove how great is my love for you."[9]

1

Arrival

April 11, 1912, was a bright, sunny morning. At the pier in New York Harbor, hundreds of people were pressed together, waiting for the arrival of the steamship *Cedric*. The 700-foot (213 m) ship had traveled from Egypt to Italy, and then crossed the Atlantic Ocean to arrive in the United States.

At that time, the only way to travel across the ocean was by ship. A year earlier, a plane built by Wilbur and Orville Wright's company had been flown across the United States, from New York to California. But regular flights to take passengers across the Atlantic wouldn't be available for another twenty-seven years.

As the *Cedric* came into view, the crowd on the pier waved their hats and handkerchiefs joyfully. They were members of the Bahá'í Faith—a religion that had been known in the United States for only about twenty years. They were eagerly awaiting one passenger—'Abdu'l-Bahá, the leader of their Faith.

The American Bahá'ís had sent thousands of dollars to help pay for 'Abdu'l-Bahá's journey. But He returned the money immediately, and took on all of the expenses Himself. Some friends had urged Him to leave the *Cedric* in Italy and travel to England, so He could sail on the maiden voyage of the magnificent new ship, the *Titanic*. But 'Abdu'l-Bahá preferred to travel simply. He made the entire trip on the *Cedric*. Later, when they learned of the *Titanic's* tragic sinking, the Bahá'ís were grateful for 'Abdu'l-Bahá's choice to remain on the *Cedric*.

Just a few years earlier, 'Abdu'l-Bahá had been allowed to leave the city of 'Akká, in what is now Israel, for the first time in forty years. Innocent of any crime, He, along with His family, had been held captive by the government because of His belief in the Bahá'í Faith, the religion founded by His Father, Bahá'u'lláh.

During all those years of injustice, 'Abdu'l-Bahá never pleaded for His freedom. He said, "I was thankful for the prison, and the lack of liberty was very pleasing to me, for those days were passed in the path of service. . . ."[1] Even though He was a prisoner in 'Akká, 'Abdu'l-Bahá cared for the poor and the sick. Many people came to Him for advice— even government officials. He wrote encouraging letters of guidance to Bahá'ís around the world, and He always put the needs of others before His own. During part of His imprisonment with His family, He slept on a mat on the floor, covered by a flea-infested blanket.

Now, at the age of sixty-seven, in poor health from years of hardship, 'Abdu'l-Bahá had arrived in the West. He was eager to meet with the Bahá'ís of North America, a group that numbered only about twelve hundred at that time. And He wanted to tell the public about the

Bahá'í teachings. Over the next eight months, He gave talks across the United States and Canada about topics such as the need to establish world peace, unity among all religions and races, and the equality of women and men.

'Abdu'l-Bahá had three people traveling with Him: His nephew, Dr. Amínu'lláh Faríd, a physician who translated 'Abdu'l-Bahá's Persian words into English; Siyyid Asadu'lláh-i-Qumí; and Maḥmúd-i-Zarqání. Maḥmúd kept a careful diary of events during the journey.

A tugboat chugged out to meet the *Cedric*, bringing newspaper reporters who wanted to interview 'Abdu'l-Bahá. He stood on the ship's upper deck. His long tan robe and black cloak flapped in the breeze. A white turban perched on His head over His long white hair. One reporter wrote, "His face was light itself as he scanned the harbor and greeted the reporters. . . ."

When the ship pulled past the Statue of Liberty, 'Abdu'l-Bahá held His arms wide and said, "There is the new world's symbol of liberty and freedom. After being forty years a prisoner I can tell you that freedom is not a matter of place. It is a condition. . . . When one is released from the prison of self, that is indeed a release."

One of the reporters asked, "What is a Bahá'í?"

'Abdu'l-Bahá replied, "To be a Bahá'í simply means to love all the world, to love humanity and try to serve it; to work for Universal Peace, and the Universal Brotherhood."[2]

Shortly after noon, the ship reached its pier. Most ocean liners docked at the Chelsea Piers, which were flanked by grand buildings with an imposing arched entrance.

Among the group of people waiting at the pier for 'Abdu'l-Bahá to go ashore was Marjory Morten, who was not yet a Bahá'í but had come with a Bahá'í named Juliet Thompson and another friend. Marjory and her husband, Alexander, were wealthy leaders in New York society. They often held gatherings at their stately home, which was filled with exquisite works of art. They also donated money to help artists, including the famous Lebanese poet, Kahlil Gibran.

Marjory and Juliet had been worried that 'Abdu'l-Bahá wouldn't like to be part of a huge public crowd. They were right. Soon a loving message came from 'Abdu'l-Bahá asking the Bahá'ís to wait to meet Him later that afternoon at the home of a Bahá'í family that lived in New York, the Kinneys.

Though she wasn't surprised, Marjory felt that even a few hours seemed too long to wait. She told her friends, "I can't leave till I've seen Him. I can't! I won't!"[3]

As the crowd drifted away from the pier and through the entrance, Marjorie and her friends found a large niche in a stone wall. They squeezed together in the spot and waited to see 'Abdu'l-Bahá leave the pier. A Bahá'í had offered his car to 'Abdu'l-Bahá. Marjory and her friends saw the car move down the street outside the pier. Suddenly, the car stopped right in front of the spot where they hid. They were sure they would be caught and would then feel embarrassed for disregarding 'Abdu'l-Bahá's wishes. But still, Marjory stubbornly refused to leave.

Finally, she saw Him. 'Abdu'l-Bahá walked through the pier entrance with His companions, and strode energetically toward the car. He radiated peace and love. His white hair and beard flowed majestically. His deep blue eyes sparkled.

Marjory later said, "From the moment I saw Him, I could not take my eyes off Him. He stopped a few yards away. I saw His face plainly. A face on which all sorrow was written, all joy. I knew then Who He was."

She turned to Juliet and whispered, "He didn't see us."[4]

But just before 'Abdu'l-Bahá got into the car, He turned toward the three hiding women and smiled directly at them.

* * *

"To be a Bahá'í simply means to love all the world, to love humanity and try to serve it; to work for Universal Peace, and the Universal Brotherhood."
— 'Abdu'l-Bahá

2

City of Love

Carrie Kinney busily prepared her large, elegant house on West End Avenue in New York, near the Hudson River, for 'Abdu'l-Bahá's arrival. She had waited three years to welcome 'Abdu'l-Bahá to her home. In 1909, when she and her husband Edward had visited Him in 'Akká with their two sons, they had asked 'Abdu'l-Bahá to stay with them when He came to America. During their eight-month visit in 'Akká, 'Abdu'l-Bahá had told them that their home would be as a heavenly constellation and that the stars would gather there.

Like stars, Bahá'ís from New York and around the world clustered at the Kinney home. The stately house provided ample room for all, and the Kinneys dedicated it to the service of the Bahá'í Faith. Even in later years when they lost some of their wealth and were forced to move to a smaller home, they still continued to hold weekly meetings for Bahá'ís and those who wanted to learn more about the Bahá'í Faith.

Edward and Carrie Kinney had attended their first Bahá'í meeting in 1895, soon after they were married. Edward accepted the Bahá'í Faith right away. He was described by a friend as robust and outgoing, with a lively sense of humor, but he was also humble and steadfast. Carrie, who had been raised a strong Catholic, was frightened by the new Faith and Edward's enthusiasm for it. When Bahá'ís came to her house, at first she was scared of them and would lock herself in the bathroom. Gradually, she grew comfortable with the Bahá'ís, and soon she realized that she too accepted the Faith's teachings. From then on, Carrie never wavered in her devoted service to the Bahá'í Faith.

When 'Abdu'l-Bahá arrived in New York, He took a suite at the Hotel Ansonia, but He held His first meeting with the Bahá'ís at the Kinney home, on the evening of April 11, 1912. He sat near a table covered with flowers, His arms around the Kinneys' two young sons, who stood at His sides. He wore a white robe and a cream-colored *fez*, a brimless hat. Several hundred people stood around the house sipping tea, and many more sat on the floor. In spite of the large group, it was quiet, with people occasionally whispering in awe and happiness.

'Abdu'l-Bahá addressed the group:

How are you? Welcome! Welcome!

After arriving today, although weary with travel, I had the utmost longing and yearning to see you and could not resist this meeting. Now that I have met you, all my weariness has vanished, for your meeting is the cause of spiritual happiness.

I was in Egypt and was not feeling well, but I wished to come to you in America. My friends said, "This is a long journey; the sea is wide; you should remain here." But the more they advised and insisted, the greater became my longing to take this trip, and now I have come to America to meet the friends of God. This long voyage will prove how great is my love for you. There were many troubles . . . but, in the thought of meeting you, all these things vanished and were forgotten.

I am greatly pleased with the city of New York. Its harbor entrance, its piers, buildings and broad avenues are magnificent and beautiful. Truly, it is a wonderful city. As New York has made such progress in material civilization, I hope that it may also advance spiritually . . . that this city may become the city of love and that the fragrances of God may be spread from this place to all parts of the world. I have come for this. I pray that you may be manifestations of the love of Bahá'u'lláh, that each one of you may become like a clear lamp of crystal from which the rays . . . may shine forth to all nations and peoples. This is my highest aspiration. . . .

It is my hope that you will all be happy and that we may meet again and again.[1]

Throughout 'Abdu'l-Bahá's journey, He spent many days at the Kinney home, meeting with groups of people large and small. The Kinneys put forth all the time, effort, and money that they could to make 'Abdu'l-Bahá's visit comfortable and pleasant. One visitor,

Howard Colby Ives, wrote that they "seemed to feel that the gift of all which they possessed was too little to express their adoring love."[2]

Howard was a minister in the Unitarian Church. He had been questioning his faith for many years, and his search had led him to some Bahá'í meetings. He was attracted to the Bahá'í teachings and read all the books he could find. And yet, his heart was troubled, and he felt very unhappy. He hoped that 'Abdu'l-Bahá would bring peace to his soul.

Howard was speaking with a Bahá'í friend and said, "When 'Abdu'l-Bahá arrives I would like very much to have a talk with Him alone, without even an interpreter."

His friend said, "I fear you couldn't get very far without an interpreter, for 'Abdu'l-Bahá speaks little English and you, I imagine, less Persian."

But Howard replied, "If He at all approaches in spiritual discernment what I hear and read of Him, we would get closer together, and I might have a better chance of understanding, even if no words were spoken."

Because there were so many visitors eager to see 'Abdu'l-Bahá that first night at the Kinney home, Howard only managed to get a glimpse of Him as he peered over someone's shoulder.

Early the next morning, Howard joined a large group of people at the Hotel Ansonia, yearning for a chance to meet 'Abdu'l-Bahá. The outer room of 'Abdu'l-Bahá's suite was filled with visitors. Telephone calls came constantly with requests for interviews and invitations to speak. Howard stood by the window, alone and silent, looking down at the busy city street below. He wondered why he was there. With so many people waiting to see 'Abdu'l-Bahá, how could he, a minister in another faith, expect to receive any attention from Him?

Then 'Abdu'l-Bahá emerged from a door, and everyone turned to look at Him. 'Abdu'l-Bahá looked up, smiled, and beckoned Howard to join Him.

Howard was startled. He wondered why 'Abdu'l-Bahá would welcome him, a stranger He had never met. He glanced around to see who 'Abdu'l-Bahá really wanted, but there was no one else standing near him to whom 'Abdu'l-Bahá might have been signaling. 'Abdu'l-Bahá beckoned again.

Slowly, Howard walked toward Him. 'Abdu'l-Bahá stretched His hand to Howard and drew him into the room. He indicated that the others in the room should leave, even the interpreter.

'Abdu'l-Bahá led Howard to the window where two chairs were waiting. Then, in English, He called Howard His own son. They sat in the chairs, and their eyes met. Howard later wrote, "It seemed as though never before had anyone really seen *me*. I felt a sense of gladness that I at last was at home. . . ."[3]

Tears flowed from Howard's eyes. 'Abdu'l-Bahá told him not to cry and said that we must always be happy. 'Abdu'l-Bahá laughed exuberantly. They sat in silence for awhile, and Howard felt extraordinary peace. Then 'Abdu'l-Bahá jumped up with another laugh and gave Howard a hug. He kissed both of Howard's cheeks, and then led him to the door. After this meeting, Howard said his life was changed forever.

Howard became a regular visitor to the Kinney home and spent as much time with 'Abdu'l-Bahá as he could. He wrote, "My ideals began to change almost from the moment of my first contact with 'Abdu'l-

Bahá." In the next few weeks, he said, "I felt like a spiritual Columbus exploring the uncharted oceans of God."[4]

Exploring a new faith was a daring act for Howard. He faced criticism from his family, friends, and other ministers. One minister joked about Howard's search, saying, "Are you still Bahá'-ing around?" A family member even told him he was ill and needed to see a doctor. But Howard felt that "the happiness unspeakable that, if only for brief moments, swept over me, repaid for all the ground abandoned."[5]

During the final days of 'Abdu'l-Bahá's visit in North America, Howard stood nearby as He was speaking with some friends. 'Abdu'l-Bahá's companion Maḥmúd said to Howard, "May I ask whether you speak from your pulpit about the Cause of Bahá'u'lláh at all?"

Howard said that he frequently quoted from the Bahá'í writings in his sermons.

"When you quote do you mention the Author?" Maḥmúd asked.

"Certainly," said Howard.

Maḥmúd said, "It must require some courage, does that not arouse criticism?"

Howard replied, "I had not thought of the matter in that light. Why should it require courage to speak of truth without regard to its source? We are not living in the middle ages."

Maḥmúd went over to 'Abdu'l-Bahá and said some words in Persian. 'Abdu'l-Bahá smiled at Howard with understanding in His intense eyes and said that it took a *great deal of courage*.[6]

Howard soon gave up his work as a minister and devoted himself to sharing the Bahá'í Faith with others. He chose jobs where he could travel and meet many people. In 1921, he and his wife, Mabel, sold or gave away all of their possessions. They took jobs as salespeople and began moving from city to city, working and holding Bahá'í meetings.

Howard wrote, "It was the ability of 'Abdu'l-Bahá to disclose their own capacity" to people that "made him the supreme Teacher and set their feet upon the straight and narrow road."[7]

* * *

"I have come to America to meet the friends of God. This long voyage will prove how great is my love for you."

— *'Abdu'l-Bahá*

3

The First Call to Peace

Just a few days after He arrived in the United States, 'Abdu'l-Bahá gave His first public talk. Juliet Thompson helped to arrange the event. Her friend Percy Grant was the minister at the Episcopal Church of the Ascension, and he invited 'Abdu'l-Bahá to give a sermon in his place.

Percy was well known in New York for supporting change. Before he became minister of the church, parishioners had followed the practice of "renting pews." They donated money in return for the privilege of sitting in a certain pew each Sunday. This was a common system at the time, and had been practiced at the Church of the Ascension for fifty years. According to *The New York Times,* it was "the most difficult church in town in which to obtain sittings."[1] Percy urged the church leaders to stop pew rental and become a "free church," in order to attract new members. Although the majority of church leaders voted in agreement with Percy, some protested passionately.

This was the first of many controversies that Percy stirred up with his innovative ideas. He also spoke out in favor of hotly debated topics such as women in the workforce, interracial marriage, and immigration. But Percy's interest in new ideas had never included support of the Bahá'í Faith. In fact, he had even warned his congregation against what he called "the Bahá'í sect."

In March 1912, Juliet was astonished and thrilled to receive a letter from Percy about 'Abdu'l-Bahá's visit, saying, "I shall be more than happy to invite him to the Ascension pulpit in my place. I should like to show so important and splendid a person, and those who love him, whatever hospitality and goodwill can be expressed. . . ."[2]

'Abdu'l-Bahá received thirteen similar invitations from churches in New York asking Him to speak—some of these invitations were even sent to Him during His ocean voyage—but He chose to accept Percy's.

On Sunday, April 14, two thousand people packed into the Church of the Ascension. Every seat was filled. It was a week after Easter, and the altar was filled with lilies, a symbol of the holy day. Percy insisted that 'Abdu'l-Bahá sit in a tall chair of honor reserved for the bishop.

Introducing 'Abdu'l-Bahá with great respect, Percy said, "I have the honor and pleasure to welcome to this place of worship a messenger from the East, freshly bearing a message of the gospel of peace, good will and love to all mankind."[3]

'Abdu'l-Bahá stood with his interpreter, Amínu'lláh Faríd, and spoke to the congregation:

Since my arrival in this country I find that material civilization has progressed greatly, that commerce has attained the utmost degree of expansion; arts, agriculture and all details of material civilization have reached the highest stage of perfection, but spiritual civilization has been left behind. Material civilization is like unto the lamp, while spiritual civilization is the light in that lamp. If the material and spiritual civilization become united, then we will have the light and the lamp together, and the outcome will be perfect. . . .

Today the world of humanity is in need of international unity and conciliation. To establish these great fundamental principles a propelling power is needed. . . . The unity of the human world and the Most Great Peace cannot be accomplished through material means. . . . The promotion of the oneness of the kingdom of humanity, which is the essence of the teachings of all the Manifestations of God, is impossible except through the divine power and breaths of the Holy Spirit. Other powers are too weak and are incapable of accomplishing this. . . .

I find a strong movement for universal peace emanating from America. It is my hope that this standard of the oneness of the world of humanity may be upraised with the utmost solidity . . . so that the world of humanity may find complete tranquillity, the eternal happiness of man become evident and the hearts of the people of the world be as mirrors in which the rays of the Sun of Reality may be reflected. Consequently, it is my request that you should strive so that the light of reality may shine and the everlasting felicity of the world of man become apparent.

I will pray for you so you may attain this everlasting happiness.[4]

The audience sat with fascinated attention while 'Abdu'l-Bahá spoke. As He walked to the exit, groups of people hurried toward Him. A woman from the crowd rushed up to Him, tears streaming down her face as she held to the hem of His robe. She was so moved that she could not speak. 'Abdu'l-Bahá calmed her with loving words.

On Monday morning, the *New York Herald* reported, "Some of the congregation . . . and members of other Episcopal churches expressed astonishment that a religious leader not professing Christianity should have been invited to preach and permitted to offer prayer within the chancel at a regular Episcopal service. . . ."[5]

But the bishop himself came to visit 'Abdu'l-Bahá and thanked Him for visiting the church. The bishop said, "I am very optimistic and pleased about the teachings of this Cause. You are the first great visitor from the East who has brought such important tidings to the West. . . . This blessed journey is the cause of praise and gratitude."[6]

* * *

"The promotion of the oneness of the kingdom of humanity, which is the essence of the teachings of all the Manifestations of God, is impossible except through the divine power and breaths of the Holy Spirit."
—*'Abdu'l-Bahá*

4

The Blessed Poor

On a snowy February night about two months before 'Abdu'l-Bahá's visit to the West, Juliet Thompson had visited the Bowery Mission. It was in a poor, neglected part of New York City, and she went there against her mother's wishes. Though she was about thirty-nine years old, it was the first time she had ever been dishonest with her mother.

The Bowery was a shelter for homeless men who had nowhere to go—they often slept in doorways or on park benches. The minister of the Bowery, Dr. Hallimond, tried to give them hope and guidance. The first two times Dr. Hallimond had invited Juliet to talk to the men who came to the Bowery Mission about the Bahá'í Faith, she had refused. Her mother didn't want her to go to the mission—perhaps because it was in an unpleasant part of the city. But when Dr. Hallimond asked a third time, Juliet couldn't bring herself to refuse. She told her mother she was having dinner with her friend Sylvia, and after dinner, the two women went to the mission.

When Juliet and Sylvia went inside, Dr. Hallimond greeted them kindly. The bitterly cold night had brought about three hundred men to the mission. Dr. Hallimond introduced Juliet, and she stood before them. As she looked out at the tired faces, she saw men who had been through difficulty and pain. Some of them looked angry and discouraged. She noticed one enormous man with white hair, who looked especially unhappy.

Juliet thought of 'Abdu'l-Bahá, who had endured so much difficulty in His life, yet was full of love and joy. She began to speak. She told the men about the Bahá'í teachings. She explained that 'Abdu'l-Bahá had been unfairly imprisoned for forty years, and had finally been released just a few years ago. Now He was traveling in the West to encourage people to love one another and establish peace.

When Juliet finished her talk, Dr. Hallimond stood. He said, "We have heard from Juliet Thompson that 'Abdu'l-Bahá will be here in April. How many of you would like to invite Him to speak at the Mission? Will those who wish it please stand?"

All three hundred men rose to their feet.

"Now," said Dr. Hallimond, "how many would like to study the thirteenth Chapter of Corinthians with Miss Thompson and myself?"

The Bible chapter he suggested was all about love. Thirty men rose, including the unhappy man with white hair.

Dr. Hallimond said, "Then we will meet every Wednesday at eight P.M. and learn something about this Love of which 'Abdu'l-Bahá is our Great Example."[1]

When Juliet got home, she told her mother what had happened that night. Her mother was so touched by the story of the men's enthusiasm that she was happy for Juliet to continue visiting the mission. Dr. Hallimond escorted Juliet safely to and from the mission each Wednesday evening.

Later, Juliet learned about the large man with white hair. His name was John Good. He had spent most of his life in jail. On the same day Juliet gave her talk, he had just been released from Sing Sing prison. He had been so disruptive there that the wardens punished him by hanging him up by his thumbs. Juliet wrote that he had left prison "full of hate and without one grain of belief in *anything*. . . ."[2] And yet, after hearing about 'Abdu'l-Bahá, he began to study the Bible each week.

'Abdu'l-Bahá once told Juliet, "You speak with a feeling, an emotion, which makes people ask: 'What is this she has?'"[3] Juliet had learned about the Bahá'í Faith while studying art in Paris. She became a Bahá'í and soon traveled to 'Akká to meet 'Abdu'l-Bahá. Later, she went to France and Switzerland to be near Him during His journeys there as well. And when He came to America, she was in His presence as much as possible.

'Abdu'l-Bahá accepted the invitation to speak at the Bowery Mission on April 19. Before His talk, He gave some money to Juliet and another Bahá'í, Edward Getsinger. He asked them to exchange the money for quarters. He told Juliet, "I want to give them some money. I am *in love* with the poor."[4]

That evening 'Abdu'l-Bahá walked toward the Bowery in His flowing robes and turban, followed by several Persian and American friends. Each of the Persian men wore a tall hat. Attracted by this unusual sight, some rowdy neighborhood boys began to bother the group. A few of them called names and threw sticks at them. Carrie Kinney, who had sons of her own, stopped and spoke with the boys as the others went ahead. She told them that 'Abdu'l-Bahá was a holy man who had been in prison for many years because of His beliefs, and He was going to speak to the poor men at the Bowery. After learning this, the boys wanted to listen too, but she invited them to hear 'Abdu'l-Bahá speak at another time.

In the chapel of the mission, Juliet and Edward each held a huge bag of quarters. They sat behind 'Abdu'l-Bahá on a platform. The long hall was packed with four hundred men. Juliet was asked to introduce 'Abdu'l-Bahá. Then He rose to speak.

Tonight I am very happy, for I have come here to meet my friends. I consider you my relatives, my companions; and I am your comrade.

You must be thankful to God that you are poor, for Jesus Christ has said, "Blessed are the poor.". . . Therefore, you must be thankful to God that although in this world you are indigent, yet the treasures of God are within your reach; and although in the material realm you are poor, yet in the Kingdom of God you are precious. Jesus Himself was poor. He did not belong to the rich. He passed His time in the desert, traveling among the poor, and lived upon the herbs of the field. He had no place to lay His head, no home. He was exposed in the open to heat, cold and frost—to inclement weather of all kinds—yet He chose this rather than riches. . . . Therefore, you are the disciples of Jesus Christ; you are His comrades, for He outwardly was poor, not rich. Even this earth's happiness does not depend upon wealth. . . . While Bahá'u'lláh was in Baghdád, still in possession of great wealth, He left all He had and went alone from the city, living two years among the poor. They were His comrades. He ate with them, slept with them and gloried in being one of them. He chose for one of His names the title of The Poor One and often in His Writings refers to Himself as *Darvish*, which in Persian means poor; and of this title He was very proud. He admonished all that we must be the servants of the poor, helpers of the poor, remember the sorrows of the poor, associate with them; for thereby we may inherit the Kingdom of heaven. . . .

So, my comrades, you are following in the footsteps of Jesus Christ. Your lives are similar to His life; your attitude is like unto His; you resemble Him more than the rich do. Therefore, we will thank God that we have been so blessed with real riches. And in conclusion, I ask you to accept 'Abdu'l-Bahá as your servant.[5]

After His talk, 'Abdu'l-Bahá stood at the door and waited for the men to walk by. Edward and Juliet stood on each side of Him, holding the big bags of quarters. The men shuffled past 'Abdu'l-Bahá, looking grimy and worn. He greeted each one like His own child. He grasped each hand and pressed some coins into the poor man's palm—sometimes five or six quarters. These men had seen little love and kindness in their lives. Sometimes they looked up at 'Abdu'l-Bahá in surprise, and seemed amazed at the love in His face. Juliet said many looked like a "drowning man rescued."[6]

When He returned to the hotel, 'Abdu'l-Bahá stopped the maid who cleaned the rooms. The day before He had given her some roses. The maid had told Juliet, "I think He is a great Saint."

There were about eighty quarters left in Juliet's bag. 'Abdu'l-Bahá asked the maid to hold out her apron. He took the bag from Juliet and poured all the quarters into the apron. Then He walked into His room.

Amazed, the maid stopped one of the men following 'Abdu'l-Bahá and said, "Oh, *see* what He has given me!" The man told her what 'Abdu'l-Bahá had done with the money at the Bowery.

The maid said, "I will do the same with this money. I will give away every cent of it."

Later that night, the maid knocked on the door of the room. She went toward 'Abdu'l-Bahá with tears in her eyes and said, "I wanted to say good-bye, Sir, and to thank You for all Your goodness to me—I never expected such goodness—and to ask You . . . to pray for me."[7]

* * *

"We must be the servants of the poor, helpers of the poor, remember the sorrows of the poor, associate with them; for thereby we may inherit the Kingdom of heaven. . . ."

— *'Abdu'l-Bahá*

5

Boys of the Bowery

The boy with dark brown skin stopped and looked up at the large, stately home of Edward and Carrie Kinney. He held back as about thirty boys—all of them white—noisily stomped up the steps. Would *he* be welcome here?

A few days earlier, Mrs. Kinney had stopped to talk with the boys outside the Bowery Mission. Some of them had been calling names and tossing sticks at a man in long robes and a white turban. They had expected Mrs. Kinney to shout and chase them away. Instead, she told them He was a holy man who was going to speak to the poor. When they asked to hear His talk, she invited them to her house instead.

The boy was curious. What was holy about the man in the long robes? And why had the lady been so nice to them? He never saw rich ladies in the neighborhood by the Bowery. And he'd never been inside a house as fine as this one. He and his companions had walked six long miles along the Hudson River to get there. Shyly, he followed the others inside.

At the time 'Abdu'l-Bahá visited America, life for kids was much different than it is now. About two million children worked at difficult and dangerous jobs in places like clothing mills, slaughterhouses, or coal mines. Thousands of kids known as "newsies" slept on the streets at night so they could wake up early and sell newspapers. Their families found they needed the kids' money in order to survive. Some of these kids were as young as five. They couldn't go to school because of their jobs. Sometimes they worked ten or more hours a day, six days a week.

However, people were beginning to realize that it was unfair to make children work. A New York photographer named Lewis Hine traveled all over the country taking pictures of kids at work, so people everywhere could see how they suffered. States began to pass laws banning child labor. By 1920, the number of working children was cut in half—but that still meant a very hard life for many kids.

We don't know the details about the boys who visited the Kinney home that day, except that they were from the poor neighborhood of the Bowery. They might have been young workers who had some time off on a spring Sunday. Or they may have been fortunate enough to go to school and live with their parents. Regardless of their circumstances, they were all greeted by 'Abdu'l-Bahá like cherished friends.

'Abdu'l-Bahá stood at the door to His room. He welcomed each boy with a smile, clasping his hand or putting an arm around him. He was friendly and full of joy.

The African American boy hesitated at the door. But when 'Abdu'l-Bahá saw him, His face lit up. He greeted the boy and exclaimed in a loud voice, "Ah, a *black* rose."

Instantly, the room was silent. The boy's face shone with happiness. He was amazed to be treated with such kindness. The other boys looked at him thoughtfully.

'Abdu'l-Bahá sent out for candy. Soon a generous five-pound box of chocolates arrived. 'Abdu'l-Bahá walked around the circle of boys and gave each one a large handful, with a kind word and a smile.

Then He picked a very dark chocolate from the box. He looked at it, then looked around at the group of boys. They all watched Him. He walked across the room to the African American boy. 'Abdu'l-Bahá's face was radiant as He affectionately put His arm around the boy. Without words, His actions seemed to say, *Your dark-skinned brother is beautiful and precious. You would love this boy as a true friend, if you would look for his inner nobility.*

Again, the room was quiet. The other boys looked at the black boy with wonder. In 1912, it was common to hear African Americans insulted and belittled. In many states, black kids were not allowed to attend school with white kids, eat in the same restaurants, or play in the same parks. Yet this fascinating man treated the black boy with respect and appreciation.

The boy himself gazed at 'Abdu'l-Bahá with admiring eyes. He seemed transformed. He looked as if all of the good qualities inside of him had instantly been revealed.

A few adults were in the room as well, and one of them, Howard Colby Ives, wondered about the effect that 'Abdu'l-Bahá's words and actions would have on the boys. He imagined what might happen if they treated people of all races with love and kindness from that moment on. Howard wrote that "freedom from just this one prejudice in the minds and hearts" of the boys "would unquestionably bring happiness and freedom from rancor to thousands of hearts."[1]

6

A Luminous Star

John Bosch walked swiftly through the cold, snowy morning to the Hotel Ansonia. He was eager to meet 'Abdu'l-Bahá, Who was staying there. The day after 'Abdu'l-Bahá arrived in New York, John took the night train from his home in Geyersville, California, and rode across the country. At that time, 'Abdu'l-Bahá didn't plan to travel to the western United States, and John didn't want to miss the chance to speak with Him.

Although some people owned cars at that time, almost all travel between cities was done by train. The first transcontinental railroad, which made it possible to travel across the country, had been completed in 1869. A couple of years earlier, George Pullman had created "hotel cars," in which travelers could sleep comfortably and dine on the train, rather than getting off of the train to buy meals. By 1910, there were 240,000 miles of train track weaving across the United States.

It was on a train that John had first learned about the Bahá'í Faith in 1903. On the way home to Geyersville from San Francisco, he met a friend, who was reading a book. He told her, "If I sit alongside of you, I'm not going to let you read—we're going to talk."

She agreed. But when she put the book down, he picked it up to take a look. It was about the teachings of 'Abdu'l-Bahá. John started to read, and he forgot all about talking to his friend. John had always been interested in religion, and after reading his friend's book about the Bahá'í Faith, he said to himself, "This is just what I wanted."

John started going to Bahá'í meetings at the home of Helen Goodall in Oakland, California. These were usually afternoon tea parties, and John was often the only man there, among up to forty-five women. In 1905, he wrote to 'Abdu'l-Bahá that he had accepted the Bahá'í Faith.

John became good friends with Thornton Chase, the first Bahá'í in the United States. Thornton worked for an insurance company in Chicago, but he often traveled to San Francisco. John and Thornton would stay at different hotels and eat dinner together. At about eleven o'clock, Thornton would say, "Now, John, I guess it's about time to take you home."

The two would walk to John's hotel, talking about the Bahá'í Faith. They would sit in the hotel parlor and continue talking. At about one o'clock, John would say, "Now, Mr. Chase, I guess it's about time to take you home." And they would walk back to Thornton's hotel.

Remembering those visits, John said, "We used to wonder what the policeman on the beat thought about us. One night we brought each other home till four in the morning."[1]

Over the years, 'Abdu'l-Bahá sent many messages to John. John was the manager of two large wineries. He had worked for years to learn the wine-making business and establish a promising career. In one Tablet, 'Abdu'l-Bahá explained that alcohol is prohibited in the Bahá'í Faith because it "leads the mind astray and is the cause of weakening the body." He told John, "I hope thou mayest become exhilarated with the wine of the love of God. . . . The after-effect of drinking is depression, but the wine of the love of God bestoweth exaltation of the spirit."[2] After receiving this message from 'Abdu'l-Bahá, John soon retired from the wine business.

At the Hotel Ansonia in New York, John booked a room for himself, then hurried to 'Abdu'l-Bahá's suite.

John recalled, "I went in as a business man. I had some questions to ask. When I saw Him I forgot everything. I was empty." As they talked, 'Abdu'l-Bahá told John everything he had wanted to know, though the questions were never asked.

John said, "'Abdu'l-Bahá, I came three thousand miles to see you."

'Abdu'l-Bahá laughed heartily and said, "I came eight thousand miles to see *you*."

John was concerned that he wasn't doing enough service to the Bahá'í Faith. He told 'Abdu'l-Bahá, "I am a foreigner, born in Switzerland, and have not the command of the English language. I would love to be a speaker. All I am doing is to give away pamphlets and as many books as are printed."

But 'Abdu'l-Bahá reassured him, "You are doing well. I am satisfied with you. With you it is not the movements of the lips, nor the tongue.

With you it is the heart that speaks. With you it is silence that speaks and radiates."[3]

Later, 'Abdu'l-Bahá got into a car that was waiting to take Him to the Kinneys' home for lunch. John saw one of 'Abdu'l-Bahá's Persian companions make a gesture in John's direction, as if pushing the air. John backed up, thinking he was being asked to go away. But this was actually the Persian gesture for "come here." Then an American gestured to John, and he understood that he was invited to join 'Abdu'l-Bahá. 'Abdu'l-Bahá took John's hand and pulled him inside the car, next to Him.

The Bahá'ís had wanted to give 'Abdu'l-Bahá a tour of New York during the drive. But John said, "He just looked at me, and all at once with an *immense* sigh . . . like the whole world would be lifted from Him so He could have a rest, He put His head on my left shoulder, clear down as close as He could, like a child, and went to sleep."

John said, "I was still as a mouse; I didn't want to move—I didn't want to wake Him up." 'Abdu'l-Bahá slept for the entire half-hour ride, and woke up just as they reached the Kinneys' home.

After lunch, 'Abdu'l-Bahá gave a talk to about 150 people. Then He walked among the group, saying good-bye, because He was leaving for Washington, D.C. John said, "You always felt a nearness to Him even when He was far across the room."[4]

John traveled with 'Abdu'l-Bahá to Washington, D.C. During that trip, 'Abdu'l-Bahá gave John a wonderful gift—a new name. 'Abdu'l-Bahá called John "Núrání." He even wrote out the name for John to see. It means "full of light" or "luminous." A few years earlier, 'Abdu'l-

Bahá had envisioned John that way. He had written in a Tablet, "Exercise on my behalf the utmost kindness and love to John D. Bosch. With the utmost humility I pray . . . that that soul may become holy, find capacity to receive the outpouring of eternity and become a luminous star in the West."[5]

7

Flowers in a Garden

On April 23, Louis Gregory eagerly joined more than one thousand people crowded into Rankin Chapel at Howard University in Washington, D.C. Louis had graduated from Howard with a law degree in 1902. He was the first African American Bahá'í who was a highly educated professional.

From its beginning, Howard University was open to both women and men of all races. It was founded just two years after the Civil War. Four million enslaved people had been freed, and most had no education. One of Howard University's goals was to train black teachers and ministers who could help blacks build better lives. Today, the university is still well known for its encouragement of African American students and culture.

At the time 'Abdu'l-Bahá visited the United States, racism was even more overt than it is today. Most African Americans lived in the South and faced harsh injustice. Though formerly enslaved people had their freedom, many whites made their lives difficult. Blacks were often denied jobs, fair wages, and voting rights. The races were separated in public schools, parks, and even on sidewalks. Signs reading "White" and "Colored" labeled separate restaurants, hotels, drinking fountains, and restrooms. In some cities, blacks walking on the street after ten P.M. were arrested. Blacks were not even allowed to *live* in several towns.

These unfair practices were actually legal. People called them "Jim Crow" laws. The name came from a stereotypical black character who was mocked by white performers in musical shows. Most Jim Crow laws were in southern states, but they could be found across the country. Some of these laws also targeted other minorities, such as Asians and American Indians.

Many southern whites also insisted that blacks treat them with special respect. African Americans often had to take off their hats and speak quietly and meekly around white people. Whites called blacks by their first names (or worse—they used racial slurs). But blacks had to call whites "sir" or "missus."

African Americans who resisted these injustices—or accidentally forgot to follow them—ran terrible risks. They might be beaten, arrested, or even killed. When arrested, blacks received longer sentences than whites, and often faced brutal prison conditions. Secret groups like the Ku Klux Klan also terrorized blacks who didn't accept the unfair conditions. They would sometimes even take revenge on the person's family members, including women and children.

When Louis Gregory was growing up in South Carolina, his family suffered due to racism and hardship. His mother and grandmother had been enslaved. His grandfather was a blacksmith who grew successful enough to own both a mule and a horse. Some local whites were offended by his success, and he was killed by the Ku Klux Klan.

In spite of these experiences, Louis and his family didn't give in to hatred or despair. Louis always saw the good in people. He wrote, "I cannot recall a time when at least some whites of the South could not be found who were willing" for blacks "to have every right and opportunity...."[1]

Louis Gregory's father died of tuberculosis when Louis was about five years old. When his mother remarried, his stepfather made sure Louis got the best education available. Schools were segregated, and the schools set up for black children were of lower quality than the white schools. But Louis was an exceptional student with a strong will to succeed. With his stepfather's help, he went on to Fisk University in Nashville, Tennessee. After his first year, Louis paid his own tuition by winning scholarships, working as a waiter, and tailoring clothes for other students (his stepfather had also helped him get trained as an apprentice tailor). In 1896, Louis became one of the very few African Americans with a college degree. He returned to Charleston, South Carolina, to work as a teacher.

But Louis had even higher ambitions. He decided to become a lawyer. Only a handful of southern schools offered law degrees to blacks, and there was no work in the South for a black lawyer. So he moved north to Washington, D.C., knowing he would never again live in the South.

Louis achieved his goals and earned his law degree from Howard University. He started to enjoy success in his new career. But he was troubled by the way African Americans were treated. He felt strongly that change was needed.

One evening, a friend asked him to attend a Bahá'í meeting. Reluctantly, as a favor for his friend, Louis went. He was impressed by the warm welcome from whites. The Bahá'í teachings about unity among all people matched his own beliefs. In 1909, Louis became a Bahá'í. Soon 'Abdu'l-Bahá gave him a huge task. He wrote to Louis, urging him to help people "close their eyes to racial differences and behold the reality of humanity. . . ."[2]

The Bahá'í community in Washington wasn't perfect. Some Bahá'ís welcomed people of all races, but others held separate meetings for whites only. Louis wrote, "Some of the friends, reading the command of Baha'u'llah which read: 'Close your eyes to racial differences and welcome all with the light of oneness,' interpreted it to mean that all barriers of race should be put aside in every meeting that was planned for teaching the Faith. Others knew the principle as wise and just, but felt that the time was not yet right for its application."[3]

These early Bahá'ís lived in a society where racial segregation was considered acceptable. In some instances, their behavior did not align with the Bahá'í teachings, which unequivocally champion the oneness of humanity. The goals of creating equity and eliminating racial prejudice continue to challenge the nation today.

Louis thought segregated meetings were wrong. He also wanted to share the Bahá'í Faith with other African Americans. He began to give public talks about the Bahá'í Faith and race unity to groups of well-educated and professional blacks. In 1910, the first formal public meeting for white and black Bahá'ís was held. The meetings continued, sometimes attended by one hundred people or more.

In 1911, Louis traveled to Egypt to see 'Abdu'l-Bahá, Who had recently been released from His forty-year imprisonment in 'Akká. Describing 'Abdu'l-Bahá, Louis wrote, "His form [was] strikingly majestic and beautiful. . . . His voice was powerful, but capable of infinite . . . tenderness and sympathy. . . . His heart . . . seemed a mysterious and boundless treasury of love feeding the hearts of all humanity."[4]

During their time together in Egypt, 'Abdu'l-Bahá encouraged Louis's efforts to build unity. He said, "All differences must fade among believers. In the present antagonism there is great danger to both races." He also explained that Bahá'í meetings should be open to people of all races. He said, "There must be no distinctions. All are equal."[5]

Soon, Louis devoted himself full-time to traveling, writing, and speaking about the Bahá'í Faith and the importance of racial unity. He gave up his legal career and turned down the opportunity to be a law professor at Howard University. Instead, he gave talks to thousands of people, traveling in the South for months at a time, often visiting black schools and universities. He said, "It is really most heartening and inspiring to see the happiness of people when they hear the Glad Tidings of the Kingdom."[6]

The efforts of Louis and other Bahá'ís to establish race unity in Washington built some trust and friendship between the races. Both white and black faculty, students, and visitors gathered in the large audience at Howard University in 1912. 'Abdu'l-Bahá was welcomed with band music and applause. The president of the university introduced Him as "the herald of love and prosperity."[7] 'Abdu'l-Bahá said:

Today I am most happy, for I see here a gathering of the servants of God. I see white and black sitting together. There are no whites and blacks before God. All colors are one, and that is the color of servitude to God. . . . If the heart is pure, white or black or any color makes no difference. God does not look at colors; He looks at the hearts. He whose heart is pure is better. He whose character is better is more pleasing. . . .

In the vegetable kingdom the colors of multicolored flowers are not the cause of discord. Rather, colors are the cause of the adornment of the garden because a single color has no appeal; but when you observe many-colored flowers, there is charm and display.

The world of humanity, too, is like a garden, and humankind are like the many-colored flowers. Therefore, different colors constitute an adornment. In the same way, there are many colors in the realm of animals. . . .

Now ponder this: Animals, despite the fact that they lack reason and understanding, do not make colors the cause of conflict. Why should man, who has reason, create conflict? This is wholly unworthy of him. . . .

I am very happy to see you and thank God that this meeting is composed of people of both races and that both are gathered in perfect love and harmony. I hope this becomes the example of universal harmony and love until no title remains except that of humanity. . . . I pray that you be with one another in utmost harmony and love and strive to enable each other to live in comfort.[8]

The audience was delighted by 'Abdu'l-Bahá's talk, and they applauded repeatedly as He spoke. Even decades later, Louis Gregory remembered 'Abdu'l-Bahá's talk as "perhaps the most powerful and impressive of all His utterances on race relations. . . ." Louis noted the "spiritual atmosphere which raised His hearers to a pitch of joyous enthusiasm." When 'Abdu'l-Bahá finished, the applause was "so long and continued" that He "felt moved to speak briefly a second time, assuring that a time would eventually come when all differences would fade."[9]

As 'Abdu'l-Bahá left the chapel, the audience stood outside in two lines, and He walked between them. The audience showed their appreciation by waving good-bye with their hats and handkerchiefs.

Louis described 'Abdu'l-Bahá's power to inspire those around Him, saying that His "Presence signalized great bounties and supreme happiness and many of the usual conventional boundaries separating races and classes seemed effaced and forgotten. He made those who sought him divinely happy."[10]

* * *

"God does not look at colors; He looks at the hearts. He whose heart is pure is better."

—*'Abdu'l-Bahá*

8

Union of East and West

'Alí Kulí Khán had planned a special luncheon and reception in honor of 'Abdu'l-Bahá at his home. Khán, as he was known, was the Chargé d'Affaires of the Persian Legation, a position similar to an ambassador. He represented the Persian (now called Iranian) government in Washington, D.C.

Khán had grown up in Tehran, Iran. As a youth, he was very bright and studious, and he was also a talented poet. He earned a college degree and was fluent in English and French. For a short time, he found work as an interpreter with a British company in Iran. But when that job ended, he couldn't find another position in which to use his talents and his knowledge of European culture. Good positions went to those who were willing to flatter, entertain, and bring gifts to the sháh and his ministers, and Khán didn't want to do this.

With little hope for a fulfilling career, Khán decided to just focus on having fun. He became friends with one of Iran's many princes. They had parties several nights a week, inviting friends to play music, dance, sing, recite poems, and tell funny stories. They even drank alcohol and smoked hashish, a drug similar to marijuana—although they were all Muslims, and this was forbidden by the Qur'án. During this time, Khán had no interest in religion.

Then Khán's brother became a Bahá'í. Not only that, but he taught many of Khán's friends about the Faith, and they became Bahá'ís, too. They stopped attending Khán's parties. Khán decided to go to the Bahá'í meetings so that he could find some faults with the Bahá'í Faith, and then persuade his friends to abandon it and return to their old ways. The meetings were held at night, in secret, because Bahá'ís were often persecuted by the Muslim authorities. In fact, Khán risked his life by going to the meetings.

In spite of his aim to challenge the Bahá'í Faith, Khán eventually began to change his mind. At first he only pretended to pay attention to the Bahá'í teachers. He even slipped out of the room now and then to drink alcohol. But Khán continued to attend these meetings for several months. He was surprised to find himself becoming interested in the Bahá'í teachings. One night he listened carefully to the stories of the Báb and Bahá'u'lláh, and they somehow touched his heart. He "rose up, took the teachers in his arms, and wept, both for joy and despair. How, he wanted to know, weak as he was, could he ever use what he had to serve Bahá'u'lláh?" The teachers told him that he would find the strength to change. Khán called that night his "resurrection from the dead."[1]

Immediately, Khán had a new goal: since he knew both Persian and English, he wanted to work for 'Abdu'l-Bahá as a translator. But he didn't have money for the long journey to 'Abdu'l-Bahá's home in 'Akká. So he dressed as a dervish, a poor wanderer who traveled on foot. He set off with two friends, each carrying a small bundle of belongings. They walked through the valleys and mountains, sleeping outside under the stars.

Through the long journey, Khán composed poems. One of his friends played music. Sometimes they stopped in towns and villages to rest their aching muscles and blistered feet. Along the way, they met Bahá'ís and taught classes about the Bahá'í Faith. They had planned to walk to India and find a way to travel by ship to 'Akká. But then they learned that Persians were no longer allowed to enter India. They were forced to head back to Tehran.

In Tehran, Khán attended many Bahá'í meetings, waiting for his chance to set out again for 'Akká. Crowds of young Bahá'ís would gather to hear Khán's stories about his time as a dervish. One night, during a blizzard, Khán impulsively said to his friends, "No more postponements, no more thoughts of preparation for the journey. Let whoever is willing, follow me!"[2]

With ten young men, Khán headed out into the snow, through the dark night, with no luggage or supplies. At midnight, they stopped at a house where travelers could rest, and they slept in their clothes. At dawn, they set out again, trudging through the deep snow. They climbed mountains and endured severe cold, with only their winter coats for bedding. After a week, they reached Rasht, a town on Iran's northern coast. They went to the governor and asked for passports to Russia. He refused. Khán's relatives had sent a telegram saying that the young men must be sent home.

The governor was a Bahá'í, but for his safety, his faith was secret from everyone except other Bahá'ís. Khán whispered to the governor, "The Bahá'í Faith has reached America and they need translations of the Sacred Writings into English. I would therefore be useful to 'Abdu'l-Bahá in 'Akká. It is urgent that I should go to Him."[3] The governor relented and gave Khán a passport. The other young men had to wait to receive money from home for the journey back to Tehran.

Khán sailed across the Caspian Sea and landed in Bákú, Azerbaijan, with about one dollar and the clothes he was wearing. He had written to 'Abdu'l-Bahá and asked for permission to visit Him, but he had not yet received an answer. He went to stay with a friend in Russia and continued to wait. Spring came, and Khán was about to go back to Iran when, finally, he received a letter from the Bahá'ís in Bákú— 'Abdu'l-Bahá had given him permission to come. Khán met up with a few other Bahá'ís, and they made a stormy, terrifying journey across the Black Sea to Constantinople (now Istanbul, Turkey). Then they waited about a week in a bug-infested inn. They were unable to go out because the Muslim authorities were suspicious of Bahá'ís, and it was dangerous for them to be seen in the city. At last, their ship was ready, and they sailed for Haifa, a city near 'Akká.

Khán had little money. On the voyage, he ate mostly bread and cheese. He and his companions slept on the open deck, sometimes in the pouring rain. After a week at sea, they reached Haifa. Once on land, Khán knelt down and kissed the ground, thanking God.

It was 1899, and four years had passed since Khán became a Bahá'í. He learned that 'Abdu'l-Bahá was in Haifa that very day. Although 'Abdu'l-Bahá was technically a prisoner in 'Akká, at times the authorities allowed Him the freedom to visit nearby Haifa. After all of K͟hán's struggles, he could hardly believe he was finally about to meet ʿAbduʾl-Bahá. He was shaking, his heart pumping wildly, as he climbed the stairs to the courtyard of the house. The instant he entered, he fell to the floor.

K͟hán was helped into another room, and a few minutes later, he felt stronger. ʿAbduʾl-Bahá sent for him, and said, "*Marḥabá! Marḥabá!* (Welcome! Welcome!) . . . You have suffered much on your wanderings, but welcome! Praise be to God, you have reached here in safety.

"The Blessed Perfection, Baháʾuʾlláh, has promised to raise up souls who would . . . assist me in spreading His Faith. . . . You, with your knowledge of English, are one of those souls promised me by Baháʾuʾlláh. You have come to assist me by translating His Sacred Writings as well as my letters to the friends in America and elsewhere in the West."

Then ʿAbduʾl-Bahá handed K͟hán some letters He had written. K͟hán saw they were in Arabic, not Persian. Panicked, K͟hán said, "In my college I studied European languages, but not Arabic!"

ʿAbduʾl-Bahá smiled lovingly and put some candy into K͟hán's hand. He said, "Go, and eat this candy. Rest assured, the Blessed Perfection will enable you to translate the Arabic into English. Rest assured that as time goes on you will be assisted to translate from the Arabic much more easily than from the Persian."[4]

After that meeting, K͟hán felt that he was filled with an indescribable new power. For more than a year, K͟hán was with ʿAbduʾl-Bahá nearly every day. It was the happiest time of his life. He rapidly wrote down letters as ʿAbduʾl-Bahá dictated them. ʿAbduʾl-Bahá gave K͟hán His own carved wooden pen case, with a silver inkpot and a small silver spoon for adding water to the powdered ink. His pens were made of thin reeds from Japan. And using dictionaries, Khán was able to translate Arabic. In years to come, he did find it easier to translate Arabic into English than his native Persian. 'Abdu'l-Bahá encouraged Khán to do his best and not to worry, because in the future, expert translators would improve on his work.

After about two years, 'Abdu'l-Bahá asked Khán to go to the United States to translate for a knowledgeable Bahá'í teacher who did not speak English, Mírzá Abu'l-Faḍl. Khán was so distressed at the thought of leaving 'Abdu'l-Bahá that he wept and beat his head against the wall. 'Abdu'l-Bahá comforted him and told him he would be doing a great service in America. He said, "I will be with you at all times. You must go forth now and give to others the bounties that have been given you here."[5]

Khán left Haifa in 1901, stopping in Paris and London before reaching the United States. He visited many Bahá'í communities with Mírzá Abu'l-Faḍl, translating for him, teaching classes, and giving his own eloquent talks.

In Boston, Khán visited the Breed family, who were interested in the Bahá'í Faith. When he entered their home, he noticed a lovely portrait of a young woman. She looked so sweet and spiritual that he thought it must be a painting of a saint. Then Florence Breed, the young woman in the portrait, walked into the room. She was a beauty who socialized in the high society of Boston. Many men had asked to marry her, but she had refused all of them because she wanted to be an actress. She studied and performed in New York and edited a magazine on the theater.

Florence and Khán spent time together over the next several weeks. When they parted, they exchanged letters. Khán taught Florence about the Bahá'í Faith, and she became a devoted Bahá'í. About a year later, they were married.

When they cabled 'Abdu'l-Bahá with the news of their marriage, He was very pleased. This was the first marriage between a Persian and American Bahá'í. 'Abdu'l-Bahá sent the couple a wonderful letter. He gave Florence the name "Rúháníyyih," which means "pure, holy, and spiritual." Later 'Abdu'l-Bahá said, "This is an evidence that the East and the West can be united and harmonized."[6]

The Kháns knew many leaders and officials in Washington. Florence served by her husband's side as hostess, welcoming distinguished guests to parties at their stately three-story home. Whenever Khán or Florence visited 'Abdu'l-Bahá, He would rise slightly, out of respect for Khán's position of leadership.

For their special luncheon in honor of 'Abdu'l-Bahá's visit to the United States, the Kháns had invited about nineteen guests to their home. Some of them held key positions in Washington politics or society. About an hour before the event, 'Abdu'l-Bahá asked Louis Gregory to meet with Him at the Kháns' home.

When luncheon was announced, 'Abdu'l-Bahá led the way into the dining room. Each person's seat at the table had been carefully arranged. There were strict rules about who should sit where, based on their positions. Since Louis wasn't invited, he waited for a chance to slip out quietly.

But when everyone had taken their places, 'Abdu'l-Bahá suddenly stood up and looked around. He said to Khán, "Where is Mr. Gregory? Bring Mr. Gregory!"

Though Louis hadn't been expected at the luncheon, <u>Kh</u>án did not argue with 'Abdu'l-Bahá. He went to find Louis. Meanwhile, 'Abdu'l-Bahá quickly rearranged the place settings that had been so carefully laid out. He gave Louis the place of honor at His right. Louis was the only African American person there. By welcoming him and giving him a prominent seat, 'Abdu'l-Bahá clearly showed that black and white people should be treated equally. He said He was very pleased to have Louis there, and He spoke about the oneness of mankind.[7]

'Abdu'l-Bahá said, "Thanks must be offered to Bahá'u'lláh because it is His confirmations that stir the souls. It is the blessings of the Abhá Beauty [Bahá'u'lláh] that change the hearts. It is the re-enforcement of the Kingdom of Abhá that makes the mosquito an eagle, the ant a Solomon, the degraded, the center of honor."[8]

Although 'Abdu'l-Bahá had spent most of His life in exile or imprisonment, sometimes in extreme poverty, He was perfectly comfortable among distinguished people and government leaders. Louis later wrote that 'Abdu'l-Bahá "made everyone feel perfectly at ease by his genial humor, wisdom and outpouring of love. . . ."[9]

9

The Titanic Disaster

Agnes Parsons had asked 'Abdu'l-Bahá to stay at her home in Washington, D.C., when He visited the United States, and He had promised to do so. This was the first home that 'Abdu'l-Bahá stayed in during His journey.

Agnes was a wealthy and dignified woman who had grown up as an only child in a prosperous home. Her husband, Jeffrey, worked at the Library of Congress in Washington, D.C., and they had two sons, Jeffrey and Royal. The Parsons were leaders in Washington society.

In 1910, when she was nearly fifty years old, Agnes visited 'Abdu'l-Bahá at His home in Haifa. She was not yet a Bahá'í, but she was curious and hopeful about the Faith.

Agnes was kept waiting for quite a while at 'Abdu'l-Bahá's home. She grew irritated. She was used to giving orders to servants in her own home, and she was accustomed to promptness. But when she finally entered 'Abdu'l-Bahá's room and their eyes met, she felt that "a ray of blinding light seemed to pass from His eyes into hers."[1] She fainted and fell to the floor.

Throughout her visit, Agnes felt that God was speaking to her. She became a strong Bahá'í who longed to serve her new Faith.

Soon after He arrived at the Parsons home, 'Abdu'l-Bahá gathered the family and their servants together. He told them that He prayed for them all. He gave each servant a handmade silk handkerchief. Mr. Parsons was not a Bahá'í, but 'Abdu'l-Bahá gave him a book of Bahá'u'lláh's writings that had been hand-copied by one of the best Persian writers.

That evening, one of 'Abdu'l-Bahá's companions cooked a Persian dinner for about twelve people. 'Abdu'l-Bahá walked around the table, serving everyone. He said, "See how good Bahá'u'lláh is to us, how great the power of His Word. From what distant parts of the world He has brought us together in this house and caused us to meet at this heavenly table. . . ."[2]

During His week in Washington, Agnes held a reception for 'Abdu'l-Bahá each evening in a long, welcoming parlor that she called "the large room." It held about two hundred people and grew more crowded each day. The walls were paneled in white, and the walls and ceiling were carved with delicate garlands. The many windows were adorned with green silk curtains. In front of the fireplace at one end of the room was a platform for 'Abdu'l-Bahá, decorated with fresh red roses. It was here that 'Abdu'l-Bahá spoke to hundreds of people—politicians, diplomats, scientists, writers, and ordinary citizens.

At one point 'Abdu'l-Bahá said to Agnes, "It is very difficult to have one like me as a guest. Every guest and traveler has a limited number of friends with whom he makes special dates for visits, but you are forced all day long to be the entertainer of all."[3]

On April 23, 'Abdu'l-Bahá and Agnes entered the Parsons home and found a crowd of about 250 people waiting. 'Abdu'l-Bahá spoke to everyone about the recent sinking of the *Titanic*, the largest ocean liner of its day.

The *Titanic* had sailed from Southampton, England, on April 10, 1912, heading to New York on its first voyage. At that time, ocean liners were a popular means of travel, and the North Atlantic route between the United States and Europe was very busy. Shipping companies competed with each other to build bigger, faster, more extravagant, and more profitable ships. The *Titanic* was famous even before it sailed. It was 852 feet long (260 m). Seven decks stretched across its vast length, like stories of a giant building. Because the hull was divided into watertight compartments, its builders claimed it was "practically unsinkable."

The *Titanic* carried about 1300 passengers, with a crew of 899. Most of the top four decks were reserved for just 300 first-class passengers. They traveled in extreme luxury, using facilities such as a gymnasium, squash court, library, Turkish bath, barber shop, and several dining rooms and restaurants. The remaining passengers had less impressive surroundings.

Sadly, the ship-building business had changed too quickly for safety regulations and other technology to keep up with it. The rudder of the *Titanic* was not designed to account for the difficulty of turning such a long ship in an emergency. Also, the ship was only required to carry sixteen lifeboats—and in fact it carried twenty—but that was still not enough for the 2,200 people aboard.

The wireless telegraph radio was still fairly new, having been in-vented at the turn of the century. The *Titanic* operators weren't ex-pected to work around the clock, and they spent much of their time sending personal messages for wealthy passengers. Still, on the evening of April 14, the *Titanic* received six wireless messages from other ships, warning of hazardous icebergs on her route. Commander Lightoller, the only senior officer to survive, wrote, "there had been an extremely mild winter in the Arctic, owing to which, ice from the ice cap and glaciers had broken away in phenomenal quantities, and official reports say that never before or since has there been known to be such quanti-ties of icebergs. . . ." Lightoller called Captain E.J. Smith "one of the ablest Skippers on the Atlantic." But for some reason, Captain Smith did not slow or stop the ship to avoid the dangerous ice.[4]

Just before midnight on April 14, the *Titanic* struck an iceberg 95 miles (153 km) south of Newfoundland, Canada. The ice ripped holes through 250 feet (76 m) of the ship's hull, and five of the watertight compartments were punctured. Shocked at the destruction of the mighty ship, passengers put on life preservers and began to flock toward the wooden lifeboats, which had a capacity of 1,178 passengers. In keeping with tradition, only women and children were put on the boats, along with enough sailors to guide them. The boats were suspended from the ship by ropes, and people carefully boarded them while they hung in midair. Then sailors lowered them to the sea.

Commander Lightoller was impressed with the courage shown by women, men, and children on the ship. Some wives refused to abandon the ship, choosing instead to stay with their husbands, facing almost certain death in the freezing water. That may help to explain why many lifeboats were only partially filled when they left the ship.

The *Titanic's* wireless radio operators continued to send distress signals until just minutes before the ship sank. A ship called the *Carpathia* received the urgent message and traveled 58 miles (93 km) to reach the survivors. Because of the ice, it was too dangerous for the *Carpathia* to move close to the lifeboats, which were spread out over a four-mile area. The exhausted survivors had to row to the ship, and it took more than four hours for everyone to be rescued. Only about 700 people survived.

As a result of the *Titanic* disaster, many advances were made in safety regulations. Each ship had to carry enough lifeboats for all passengers and crew, and to hold lifeboat drills, so everyone would know what to do in an emergency. Constant radio contact was required during a voyage. And the International Ice Patrol was established, to report iceberg dangers to ships in the North Atlantic.

Some Bahá'ís had urged 'Abdu'l-Bahá to sail on the *Titanic*. It was suggested that He leave His ship, the *Cedric,* when it stopped in Italy, and travel to England to board the faster, larger ship. But 'Abdu'l-Bahá had said, "No, we will go direct, trusting in the assistance and protection of the Blessed Beauty. He is the true Protector and the divine Keeper."[5] When they learned of the *Titanic's* fate, the Bahá'ís said prayers of gratitude that 'Abdu'l-Bahá had not taken their suggestion.

'Abdu'l-Bahá joined the rest of the world in mourning for the sad loss of 1,500 lives. In His talk to the crowd at the Parsons home, He offered spiritual comfort:

Within the last few days a terrible event has happened in the world, an event saddening to every heart and grieving every spirit. I refer to the Titanic disaster, in which many of our fellow human beings were drowned, a number of beautiful souls passed beyond this earthly life. . . . Some of those who were lost voyaged on the Cedric with us as far as Naples and afterward sailed upon the other ship. When I think of them, I am very sad indeed. But when I consider this calamity in another aspect, I am consoled by the realization that the worlds of God are infinite; that though they were deprived of this existence, they have other opportunities in the life beyond. . . .

These human conditions may be likened to the matrix of the mother from which a child is to be born into the spacious outer world. At first the infant finds it very difficult to reconcile itself to its new existence. It cries as if not wishing to be separated from its narrow abode and imagining that life is restricted to that limited space. It is reluctant to leave its home, but nature forces it into this world. Having come into its new conditions, it finds that it has passed from darkness into a sphere of radiance; from gloomy and restricted surroundings it has been transferred to a spacious and delightful environment. . . . This analogy expresses the relation of the temporal world to the life hereafter. . . . At first it is very difficult to welcome death, but after attaining its new condition the soul is grateful. . . . It has been freed from a world of sorrow, grief and trials to live in a world of unending bliss and joy. . . . [6]

Juliet Thompson described this meeting in her diary. She said that 'Abdu'l-Bahá strode "back and forth with a step so vibrant it shook you." She described His eyes as "piercing our souls" and said that He filled the room with "a mysterious energy."[7]

Later that summer, 'Abdu'l-Bahá met a woman who had survived the *Titanic* tragedy. She said, "I am told that you advised not to travel by that ship."

'Abdu'l-Bahá told her that was true.

"Did you know that this would happen?" she asked.

'Abdu'l-Bahá responded, "God inspires man's heart."[8]

* * *

"At first it is very difficult to welcome death, but after attaining its new condition the soul is grateful. . . . It has been freed from a world of sorrow, grief and trials to live in a world of unending bliss and joy."

— 'Abdu'l-Bahá

10

Pure Hearts

'Abdu'l-Bahá dearly loved children. He said, "There is nothing more delightful than the emotion one feels in embracing a sweet child, it makes one's very ribs dilate."[1] Marzieh, the daughter of Florence and Ali-Kuli Khán, was four years old at the time of 'Abdu'l-Bahá's journey to North America. With an adult's help, she wrote to Him, "Dear 'Abdu'l-Bahá, I love you. I hope you will come to see us." 'Abdu'l-Bahá replied by writing a message related to the meaning of her name: "O God, make her who is pleasing to God (Marzieh), well-pleased with God (Razieh). Inshá'lláh [God willing] I shall see her."[2] He signed the note and sent it back to her.

The Khán family had been among the few Bahá'ís waiting to greet 'Abdu'l-Bahá at the train station in Washington, D.C. As with His arrival in New York, He wanted to avoid a large public scene. Florence Khán bought flowers for her children to give Him—red roses from Marzieh, and violets from her older brother, Rahim, who was about six. 'Abdu'l-Bahá held Marzieh on His lap in the car. When Florence peered at them through the window, 'Abdu'l-Bahá pointed to Marzieh, and His "smile was so happy and loving that Florence could not believe it was for her."[3]

'Abdu'l-Bahá often played with Marzieh, tugging at her curls affectionately as He talked with adults around them. Florence said, "Marzieh stuck to Him like . . . plaster."[4] Years later, Marzieh remembered "an atmosphere about Him, an electric feeling of something always going on."[5] She also wrote, "With Him, there was room for every one, no matter how heavy His own work load, or how weary His body, no matter how small the person was, or how unnoticed by the world."[6]

'Abdu'l-Bahá agreed to have His photo taken with Marzieh, Rahim, and their younger sister, Hamideh. Florence carefully dressed them in their best clothing. The photographers arranged the three children around 'Abdu'l-Bahá. He put His arms around Hamideh, and gave her some candy. The children had to hold very still. There was a bright flash of light and a loud noise as the explosive flash powder was lit. A puff of smoke followed, and the moment had been preserved on film.

Another Washington child who enjoyed 'Abdu'l-Bahá's attention was Agnes Parsons's younger son, who was named Jeffrey, like his father. 'Abdu'l-Bahá and Jeffrey looked at the boy's toys, books, and pictures, and they went to the roof garden of the Parsonses home. 'Abdu'l-Bahá also gave Jeffrey a Persian inkwell.

The Washington Bahá'ís held a weekly Sunday school at Studio Hall, the home and gallery of Alice Barney-Hemmick. Alice was the mother of a Bahá'í woman and was supportive of the Bahá'í community.

She was also an accomplished painter and a patron of the arts in Washington.

On April 24, more than one hundred children gathered at Studio Hall for a special meeting with 'Abdu'l-Bahá. One observer called this "one of the most beautiful functions of the week. . . ."[7] The meeting opened with songs by the children. He gave each one a piece of candy and said, "Praise be to God! These children are like a bouquet of roses in their utmost beauty, delicacy and sweetness."[8] Then He spoke to the children, along with their parents and other visitors:

What a wonderful meeting this is! These are the children of the Kingdom. The song we have just listened to was very beautiful in melody and words. The art of music is divine and effective. It is the food of the soul and spirit. Through the power and charm of music the spirit of man is uplifted. It has wonderful sway and effect in the hearts of children, for their hearts are pure, and melodies have great influence in them. . . . It is incumbent upon each child to know something of music, for without knowledge of this art the melodies of instrument and voice cannot be rightly enjoyed. . . .

Today illumined and spiritual children are gathered in this meeting. . . . They have pure hearts. They have spiritual faces. . . . That is why Christ has addressed the world, saying, "Except ye be converted, and become as little children, ye shall not enter into the kingdom of heaven"—that is, men must become pure in heart to know God. . . . The hearts of all children are of the utmost purity. . . .

I pray in behalf of these children . . . so that each one may be trained under the shadow of the protection of God, each may become like a lighted candle in the world of humanity. . . . that they may become characterized with such virtues, perfections and qualities that their mothers, fathers and relatives will be thankful to God, well pleased and hopeful. . . .

. . . Therefore, make ye an effort in order that these children may be rightly trained and educated and that each one of them may attain perfection in the world of humanity. Know ye the value of these children, for they are all my children.[9]

After 'Abdu'l-Bahá's talk, each child calmly and politely walked forward to meet Him. He embraced and blessed each one lovingly. But when it was Marzieh <u>Kh</u>án's turn, she "exploded from her chair, bolted to Him, ran between His knees, banged her head against His breast, and then bolted back," as the audience chuckled at her enthusiasm.[10]

Agnes Parsons urged her son Jeffrey to greet 'Abdu'l-Bahá, too. But Jeffrey said, "I live in the house with Him."

Agnes said, "You would like to do what the others are doing, would you not?"

So Jeffrey went forward, and 'Abdu'l-Bahá hugged him. Jeffrey returned to his mother with "flushed cheeks and radiant eyes." He said, "It is like Jesus and the little children."[11]

* * *

"Know ye the value of these children, for they are all my children."
— *'Abdu'l-Bahá*

11

Suffering and Glory

'Abdu'l-Bahá met many influential leaders in Washington, D.C., who treated Him with great respect. These distinguished people included the inventor of the telephone, Alexander Graham Bell; former president Theodore Roosevelt; Admiral Robert Peary, who had just returned from exploring the North Pole; Mabel Boardman, National Secretary of the American Red Cross; Lee McClung, Secretary of the United States Treasury; and Ḍíyá Páshá, the Ambassador of Turkey.

Alexander Graham Bell was so impressed with 'Abdu'l-Bahá that he invited Him to join a meeting of leading scientists at his home. At the gathering, several of the scientists spoke about their research and discoveries. Then Alexander invited 'Abdu'l-Bahá to speak. 'Abdu'l-Bahá praised the group and spoke about the importance of science and the greatness of the modern age. 'Abdu'l-Bahá's companion Maḥmúd said that Alexander was "extremely delighted" with this talk. "The hearts of those present were so moved that when the next member arose to give his talk, he could only say, 'The talk of the Master from the East was so wonderful that I find myself inadequate to say anything.'"[1]

Later, 'Abdu'l-Bahá spoke with Alexander's wife and daughter. Because his wife was deaf, Alexander used sign language to translate. He explained that the telephone was the result of his efforts to create a tool to help the deaf communicate. He had been inspired by his deep love for his wife.

The admiration showered on 'Abdu'l-Bahá from people of all walks of life made a remarkable contrast to the sorrows His Father, Bahá'u'lláh, had endured in earlier years. When 'Abdu'l-Bahá was a child of eight, Bahá'u'lláh had been chained in a horrible dungeon in Tehran, Iran, in officials' efforts to stop the new Faith. While Bahá'u'lláh suffered under the weight of massively heavy chains, His home was ransacked, and His family was thrust into poverty. At times 'Abdu'l-Bahá had only a handful of dry flour for food. 'Abdu'l-Bahá and His family shared in Bahá'u'lláh's many trials, as He was exiled from His homeland and eventually confined in the army barracks of 'Akká.

Describing 'Abdu'l-Bahá's experiences in the West, His grandson Shoghi Effendi wrote, "pictures from the tragic past such as these must have many a time overpowered Him with feelings of mingled gratitude and sorrow, as He witnessed the many marks of respect, of esteem, and honor now shown Him and the Faith which He represented."[2]

One evening, as 'Abdu'l-Bahá was driven through Washington, He poured out His heart in a loud, ringing voice:

O Bahá'u'lláh! What hast Thou done? O Bahá'u'lláh! May my life be sacrificed for Thee! O Bahá'u'lláh! May my soul be offered

up for Thy sake! How full were Thy days with trials and tribula-
tions! How severe the ordeals Thou didst endure! How solid the
foundation Thou hast finally laid, and how glorious the banner
Thou didst hoist![3]

Another time, when 'Abdu'l-Bahá was speaking of His Father's
sufferings, "He was so overcome with emotion that He sobbed aloud
in His grief. . . . All His attendants wept with Him, and were plunged
into sorrow as they heard the tale of the woeful trials endured by the
Ancient Beauty [Bahá'u'lláh], and witnessed the tenderness of heart
manifested by His Son."[4]

For many years, the government of Turkey had persecuted and
imprisoned Bahá'u'lláh and His family. Still, when 'Abdu'l-Bahá met
the Turkish ambassador, Ḍíyá Páshá, the ambassador listened to Him
with careful attention. He became a great admirer of 'Abdu'l-Bahá,
visiting Him frequently and attending some of His talks. 'Abdu'l-Bahá
often invited the ambassador to join Him on drives in Washington.

Ḍíyá Páshá even held a banquet in 'Abdu'l-Bahá's honor at the
Turkish Embassy on April 25. Many government officials attended.
Two footmen in uniform opened the doors as 'Abdu'l-Bahá arrived
with Florence and Ali-Kuli Khán. 'Abdu'l-Bahá spoke to them kindly
in Turkish. Inside, hundreds of roses were strewn on the tables, and
piled into a mound at the places of 'Abdu'l-Bahá and Ḍíyá Páshá.

The ambassador praised 'Abdu'l-Bahá before all the guests, saying,
"The light of His honor's quality and knowledge . . . is now shining
upon all peoples, showering them with His encouragement and en-
lightenment. He has suffered and sacrificed everything for the purpose

of disseminating good qualities for humanity. He has now honored us by His presence. His Honor, 'Abdu'l-Bahá, is unique in our age and is highly esteemed and treasured by all of us. With prayer to the Lord of the worlds, I wish Him a long life and good health."[5]

In response, 'Abdu'l-Bahá humbly replied, "I am not worthy of this." Then He addressed the gathering:

Tonight is a blessed night, worthy of rejoicing and thanksgiving for several reasons. First, thanks be to God, we are in a country that is most prosperous and free. Second, at a home which is related to the sublime Turkish Empire. Third, we are the guests of His Excellency, the Ambassador, who is in the realm of morals shining like the sun. Fourth, this meeting portrays the unity and harmony of the East and the West. . . . Undoubtedly the utmost desire of the people of . . . broad ideas and sound minds, is love amongst human beings; their highest hope is for unity and harmony amongst mankind. . . .The members of the human family are in reality one; all are from one family, of one country and of one globe. This is the age of the oneness of mankind and the passing away of superstitions of past centuries. Every thoughtful person feels that this is the century of oneness and unity, and the imaginary prejudices are vanishing. Therefore, we are hopeful that the misunderstandings amongst the nations may disappear. . . .

I am thankful and grateful for the kindness of His Excellency the Ambassador, because he was the cause of gathering and uniting different people in this meeting. Undoubtedly such meetings are worthy of thanks and praise.[6]

Several times throughout the night, Ḍíyá Páshá had tears in his eyes as he watched 'Abdu'l-Bahá. At one point he said to Juliet Thompson, "Truly, He is a Saint."[7] When the meeting ended, the ambassador walked with 'Abdu'l-Bahá to His carriage, showing humble appreciation.

Before 'Abdu'l-Bahá left Washington, Agnes Parsons offered Him a large sum of money to help with the expenses of His trip. 'Abdu'l-Bahá gently asked her to give the money to the poor instead.

Many friends came to the train station to see 'Abdu'l-Bahá once more as He departed for Chicago. He told Agnes, "This was the springtime; we had good meetings at your home; I shall never forget them. I shall pray for divine confirmation for you that you may be assisted both materially and spiritually."

He told the other friends, "I hope these meetings of ours will bring forth everlasting results. The greatest of all benefits is the oneness of humanity and universal peace."[8]

12

Temple of Unity

When 'Abdu'l-Bahá arrived in Chicago on April 29, He told the Bahá'ís, "You have a beautiful city. . . . Just as this city is lighted with electric light, I hope that it may become lighted with the Light of the Kingdom. . . . I like Chicago very much, for the call of Bahá'u'lláh was first raised in this city."[1]

Chicago became the first city in the United States to mention the Bahá'í Faith in 1893, at a huge fair called the World's Columbian Exposition. The event had rides, music, art galleries, science exhibits, cultural displays, and meetings on topics of the day. It also had the world's first Ferris wheel—which held more than 2,000 riders! Millions of people attended the fair during the six months it was open.

A fascinating part of the fair was the World's Parliament of Religions. For the first time, Christians, Jews, Muslims, Hindus, Buddhists, and people from other faiths gathered to learn from each other. The Bahá'í Faith was included in a report from a Christian minister who had been

living in the Middle East. Although he misunderstood the Bahá'í
teachings, he did share this quote from Bahá'u'lláh:

That all nations should become one in faith and all men as brothers; that the bonds of affection and unity between the sons of
men should be strengthened; that diversity of religion should
cease and differences of race be annulled; what harm is there in
this? Yet so it shall be. These fruitless strifes, these ruinous wars
shall pass away, and the 'Most Great Peace' shall come.[2]

Parts of the missionary's report were also printed in Chicago
newspapers. Soon after, a Middle Eastern Bahá'í came to Chicago and
began teaching Bahá'í classes. The following year, a man who lived in
Chicago named Thornton Chase became the first American Bahá'í. By
1899, about seven hundred Bahá'ís were living in Chicago.

One Chicago woman who made a lasting contribution to the Bahá'í
community was Corinne True. Corinne and her husband Moses
suffered many tragedies in their family life. When Corinne was thirty,
their daughter, who was nearly nine, died from a falling accident.
Several years later, four of Corinne's children became very ill with
diphtheria, a disease that causes breathing problems and heart damage.
Today, due to vaccinations, diphtheria is extremely rare. But at that
time, no vaccinations or antibiotics were available, and diphtheria took
thousands of lives each year. Corinne nursed the ill children for months.
The older children recovered, but three-year-old Nathanael died.

Corinne had been raised as a Christian—her father was a Presbyterian
minister. But in her grief at losing her children, she began to search for

new spiritual comfort. One day, a friend who had been to an inspiring Bahá'í lecture suggested that Corinne attend. Corinne did. She immediately said to herself, "This is it." When she got home, her husband, Moses, knew she had found the faith she needed.

Like most new Bahá'ís at that time, Corinne wrote to 'Abdu'l-Bahá. He answered her with comfort about Nathanael: "Be not grieved nor troubled because of the loss which hath befallen thee. . . . know that thy pure son shall be with thee in the Kingdom of God and thou shalt witness his smiling face, illumined brow, handsome spirit and real happiness."[3]

A few weeks later, another outbreak of diphtheria hit Chicago. Corinne's seven-year-old twins, Katherine and Kenneth, became seriously ill. Corinne prayed for them and read 'Abdu'l-Bahá's letter often. Katherine recovered, but Kenneth passed away. Another message from 'Abdu'l-Bahá gave Corinne strength. He wrote, "Know thou, that thy beloved son hath soared, with the wing of soul, up to the loftiest height which is never-ending in the Kingdom of God. . . . Wert thou informed of the position in which is thy son, thy face would be illumined by the lights of happiness. . . ."[4]

Corinne's new faith helped her to endure the loss of another child. She also comforted Moses and their remaining five children. Everyone was amazed at her strength.

Soon Corinne began to devote much of her time and energy to the Bahá'í Faith. Moses supported her, and he never complained about her being away from the family for meetings. Although Corinne was grateful for his kindness, she longed to share the Bahá'í Faith with Moses. 'Abdu'l-Bahá sent a prayer for Corinne to say for her husband:

O my Lord! Make the eyes of my husband to see. Rejoice Thou his heart with the light of the knowledge of Thee, draw Thou his mind unto Thy luminous beauty, cheer Thou his spirit by revealing unto him Thy manifest splendors.

O my Lord! Lift Thou the veil from before his sight. Rain down Thy plenteous bounties upon him, intoxicate him with the wine of love for Thee, make him one of Thy angels whose feet walk upon this earth even as their souls are soaring through the high heavens. Cause him to become a brilliant lamp, shining out with the light of Thy wisdom in the midst of Thy people.

Verily Thou art the Precious, the Ever-Bestowing, the Open of Hand.[5]

In 1903, some Chicago Bahá'ís learned that work had begun on the first Bahá'í Temple in the world, in far-away 'Ishqábád, in what is now Turkmenistan. Immediately, they wrote to 'Abdu'l-Bahá and asked permission to build a Temple in the United States. He approved their request. Shortly afterward, 'Abdu'l-Bahá wrote to Corinne, "Whosoever arises for the service of this building shall be assisted with a great power from His Supreme Kingdom and upon him spiritual and heavenly blessings shall descend. . . ."[6]

Over the next few years, the Bahá'ís began to contribute funds for the Temple. Then, in 1906, the Chicago Bahá'ís made an effort to unify Bahá'ís around the country in support of the project. They sent a petition to all the Bahá'ís in North America, asking them to sign if they wished to help build the Temple. Nearly eight hundred signatures were collected. Moses True compiled them on a scroll to be delivered to 'Abdu'l-Bahá.

That same year, Corinne and Moses lost their oldest son, Laurence, when he drowned in a sailing accident. Again, Corinne's faith gave her the strength to console her family. She received another comforting letter from 'Abdu'l-Bahá. This time, Corinne was filled with a strong desire to meet 'Abdu'l-Bahá. Though she feared long-distance travel, she asked His permission to journey to 'Akká with her daughter, Arna, who was about sixteen. Corinne was entrusted with the Temple petition, along with a suitcase full of letters, photos, and gifts from many Bahá'ís—including a shawl, a fruitcake, and a crocheted mat.

When Corinne and Arna arrived in 'Akká, 'Abdu'l-Bahá welcomed them warmly, bringing a bouquet of purple and pink hyacinths. Corinne said, "I found Him to be a powerful Dynamo—a Lion—as well as the Most Majestic Personage I ever hope to see."[7]

The next day, Corinne and Arna met with 'Abdu'l-Bahá. Corinne put the scroll on the sofa and began giving Him the gifts and photos from the Bahá'ís. But before she could present the scroll, He walked across the room, reached for it, and held it up in the air. "This is what gives me great joy," He said. "Go back and work for the Temple; it is a great work." He told Corinne that she had done well, and that she was His own daughter.[8]

'Abdu'l-Bahá gave Corinne instructions about the Temple. He said it should be built on the shore of Lake Michigan, away from the business district of Chicago. He said the building should have nine sides, and be surrounded by nine gardens, with a fountain in each. He looked intensely at Corinne and said, "Devote yourself to this project—make a beginning, and all will come right."⁹

When Corinne returned home, she immediately wrote letters to Bahá'ís around the country, explaining the importance of the Temple project. Soon contributions began to arrive. For many weeks, she and a friend traveled by horse-drawn streetcar to the north of Chicago, then hiked through fields, seeking land for the Temple. Finally, she found a site in what is now Wilmette, Illinois, and felt it was "the chosen place." In 1908, the Bahá'ís purchased about a half acre of the land and began to gather there occasionally.

Corinne wrote to 'Abdu'l-Bahá, suggesting that a group made up of Bahá'ís from around the country should make decisions about the Temple. He approved, and the Bahá'í Temple Unity was formed in 1909. Corinne served as its financial secretary for thirteen years.

Moses found real joy in serving others at his wife's side. He was naturally outgoing, and he was happy to welcome people of all faiths and backgrounds into their home. He didn't openly declare his belief in the Bahá'í Faith. But in late 1909, while the Trues were hosting a Bahá'í gathering, Moses said to a guest, "If the Revelation is as you say it is . . . then I am a Bahá'í."¹⁰

Corinne and her daughters noticed that Moses was especially joyful during the next two weeks, but they could tell he was physically weak. Then one morning, he had a sudden heart attack and passed away. Corinne grieved for her husband, but as always, her faith sustained her. She urged her children to think about the progress of their father's soul rather than their own sadness.

Corinne continued to work enthusiastically on the Temple project. Because of her tireless and passionate work, Bahá'ís around the world came to affectionately call her "Mother of the Temple." Corinne received strength and guidance from more than fifty letters sent to her by 'Abdu'l-Bahá throughout her life.

On the morning of April 30, 1912, 'Abdu'l-Bahá's second day in Chicago, He learned that Corinne True's son Davis was seriously ill. He immediately left the hotel for her home.

'Abdu'l-Bahá spent a long time with Davis. Then He walked across the hall to another room. He paced back and forth across the room, and repeatedly cried out fervently, "The calamities in this house must cease."[11]

When He went downstairs, 'Abdu'l-Bahá told Corinne that Davis was much better than expected. She was thrilled, and felt sure that her son would recover. At 'Abdu'l-Bahá's invitation, Corinne joined Him while He gave three speeches that day.

First 'Abdu'l-Bahá spoke at a community center called Hull House, which provided adult classes, child care, children's activities, a library, and many other services for the poor of Chicago. After His talk, 'Abdu'l-Bahá stood among the crowd of children and adults, and gave each person a quarter or half-dollar.

Hull House had been co-founded by Jane Addams, who was well known as a writer, speaker, and promoter of international peace. In 1931, she became the first American woman to receive the Nobel Peace Prize. Today, the Jane Addams Hull House Association serves 60,000 people from dozens of sites throughout the Chicago area.

Next, 'Abdu'l-Bahá spoke to the Fourth Annual Conference of the NAACP (National Association for the Advancement of Colored People). The NAACP was founded in 1909 to help stop injustice toward African Americans in the United States. It was supported by people of many backgrounds, including Jane Addams and the noted scholar and writer W.E.B. DuBois. Today, the NAACP continues to promote racial equality worldwide.

Finally, in the evening, 'Abdu'l-Bahá addressed more than one thousand people at a meeting of the Bahá'í Temple Unity. 'Abdu'l-Bahá explained the importance of the Temple. He called it the Mashriqu'l-Adhkár, an Arabic term that means "the dawning place of the mention of God":

> The original purpose of temples and houses of worship is simply that of unity—places of meeting where various peoples, different races and souls of every capacity may come together in order that love and agreement should be manifest between them. That is why Bahá'u'lláh has commanded that a place of worship be built for all the religionists of the world; that all religions, races and sects may come together within its universal shelter; that the proclamation of the oneness of mankind shall go forth from its open courts of holiness—the announcement that humanity is the servant of God and that all are submerged in the ocean of His mercy. It is the Mashriqu'l Adhkár. . . .
>
> I pray in your behalf that your hearts may be enlightened with the light of the love of God; that your minds may develop daily;

that your spirits may become aglow with the fire and illumination of His glad tidings, until these divine foundations may become established throughout the human world. . . .

O Thou kind Lord! This gathering is turning to Thee. These hearts are radiant with Thy love. These minds and spirits are exhilarated by the message of Thy glad tidings. O God! Let this American democracy become glorious in spiritual degrees even as it has aspired to material degrees, and render this just government victorious. Confirm this revered nation to upraise the standard of the oneness of humanity, to promulgate the Most Great Peace, to become thereby most glorious and praiseworthy among all the nations of the world. O God! This American nation is worthy of Thy favors and is deserving of Thy mercy. Make it precious and near to Thee through Thy bounty and bestowal.[12]

After 'Abdu'l-Bahá's talk, the audience sang "Temple Song," composed by a Bahá'í musician named Louise Waite. 'Abdu'l-Bahá then gave a financial gift to the Temple Fund.

When Corinne returned home, she realized that when 'Abdu'l-Bahá had told her that her son was better than expected, He must have been talking about Davis's spiritual health. While she was out, Davis had passed away peacefully. Corinne was comforted to learn that a few moments before he died, Davis had whispered, "O 'Abdu'l-Bahá! I love you! I love you!"[13]

* * *

"The original purpose of temples and houses of worship is simply that . . . different races and souls of every capacity may come together in order that love and agreement should be manifest between them."

—*'Abdu'l-Bahá*

13

The Cornerstone

On May 1, 1912, a large tent was set up on the Temple grounds in Wilmette, Illinois. Almost four hundred Bahá'ís gathered there, waiting for 'Abdu'l-Bahá to arrive. Although her son Davis had died just the day before, Corinne True was among the crowd. Nothing could keep her away from 'Abdu'l-Bahá.

One Bahá'í who had made a significant contribution to the Temple was not able to attend that day—Esther Tobin, known as "Nettie" to her friends. Nettie was a widow who lived near downtown Chicago with her two sons, John and Harold. She worked hard as a dressmaker, but she had trouble making enough money to support her family. Often she purchased food for their evening meal with the money she had earned that day. She prayed every day for God's help and guidance.

Then Nettie met a Bahá'í named Paul Dealy. Nettie attended his classes about the Bahá'í Faith, and she felt that her prayers had been answered. She became a Bahá'í around 1903. Nettie also met Corinne

True, and Corinne hired her as a dressmaker. Nettie went to the True home to work every week.

Nettie was unhappy that she wasn't able to contribute money to the Bahá'í Temple. Bahá'ís from throughout the United States were sending money to Corinne True for the project. In time, contributions also came from Canada, Mexico, Hawaii, Europe, India, Russia, Africa, the Middle East, South America, and New Zealand. 'Abdu'l-Bahá encouraged this demonstration of world unity.

Nettie prayed and asked God to send her something she could offer as a gift to the Temple. She said that one day in 1908, she was working alone when she heard a voice say, "Do you believe in immortality?" Nettie answered, "Yes, I do." The voice said, "Then, get a stone."

A few days later, Nettie heard the voice again, even louder: "Do you believe in immortality?" Nettie said, "Yes, I do." And the voice repeated, "Get a stone." [1]

Later, Nettie heard the same command again. This time, she was inspired to follow it. She went to a construction site near her home and spoke to the foreman. She told him about the Temple and asked if she could buy an inexpensive building stone. The foreman showed her a pile of damaged limestone rocks that couldn't be used for building, and he said she could have one.

Later that day, with help from a neighbor, Nettie wrapped one of the stones in a piece of carpet, tied a clothesline around it, and dragged it to her home. Two days later, Nettie asked for help from Mírzá Husayn Mazlúm, an elderly Persian Bahá'í. With Nettie's brother Leo, they began the journey north to the Temple site. When they tried to board a horse-drawn streetcar, the conductor didn't want them to bring the stone on board, but Nettie insisted, and he gave in. They hefted the stone onto the back platform of the car and traveled through Chicago. On the north side of the city, they transferred to another car and rode to Evanston. When they left the streetcar, they were still six blocks away from the Temple land. They carried the stone for three blocks, then it became too heavy, and they dragged it along the ground.

Corinne True and another friend had been waiting at the Temple site for Nettie and her companions to arrive. As the day dragged on, they became worried and set out to find them. When they met, Mírzá Mazlúm asked the others to put the stone on his back. He carried it for another half of a block. Then, exhausted, the group left the stone in an old, abandoned farmhouse overnight.

Early the next morning, Nettie appeared at the farmhouse with a homemade cart and a shovel. When she tried to lift the stone into the cart, she broke the cart's handle and hurt her wrist. A man nearby helped her put the stone in the cart and fixed the handle. Nettie managed another half of a block. Then she met a boy who helped her get to the corner of the Temple land and drag the cart across it. The cart fell apart, and the stone was left sitting in the rubble. Nettie said some prayers and returned home.[2]

Nettie Tobin's stone became a focal point for gatherings at the Temple site. Although 'Abdu'l-Bahá had sent a stone marker to the United States, and some Bahá'ís around the world did the same, none of those stones ever made it to the grounds. In the words of the Bible, "The stone which the builders rejected has become the chief corner stone."[3]

On May 1, 'Abdu'l-Bahá was expected to arrive at the Temple land at 11:00 A.M., but it was 1:00 P.M. when His taxi was finally spotted. The taxi stopped on the road, and one of 'Abdu'l-Bahá's Persian companions called for Corinne. She joined Him in the cab, and they drove around to the other side of the property. After a short time, some children saw 'Abdu'l-Bahá and Corinne walking together toward the tent. The children ran to them, and 'Abdu'l-Bahá greeted them lovingly.

When 'Abdu'l-Bahá entered the tent on the Temple site, He stood in the center of the group and paced back and forth as He spoke to the crowd:

The power which has gathered you here today notwithstanding the cold and windy weather is, indeed, mighty and wonderful. It is the power of God, the divine favor of Bahá'u'lláh which has drawn you together. . . .

Thousands of Mashriqu'l-Adhkárs, dawning points of praise and mention of God for all religionists will be built in the East and in the West, but this, being the first one erected in the Occident, has great importance. In the future there will be many here and elsewhere—in Asia, Europe, even in Africa, New Zealand and Australia—but this edifice in Chicago is of especial significance. It has the same importance as the Mashriqu'l-Adhkár in 'Ishqábád . . . the first one built there. . . . The Mashriqu'l-Adhkár in 'Ishqábád is almost completed. It is centrally located, nine avenues leading into it, nine gardens, nine fountains; all the arrangement and construction is according to the principle and proportion of the number nine. It is like a beautiful bouquet. Imagine a very lofty, imposing edifice surrounded completely by gardens of variegated flowers, with nine avenues leading through them, nine fountains and pools of water. Such is its matchless, beautiful design. Now they are building a hospital, a school for orphans, a home for cripples, a hospice and a large dispensary. God willing, when it is fully completed, it will be a paradise.

I hope the Mashriqu'l-Adhkár in Chicago will be like this.[4]

When He finished speaking, 'Abdu'l-Bahá left the tent and asked for Nettie's stone to be brought to Him. Irene Holmes, a Bahá'í from New York, handed 'Abdu'l-Bahá a leather case holding a golden trowel. 'Abdu'l-Bahá tried to use the trowel to dig a spot for the cornerstone, but it wasn't strong enough to cut through the ground. He asked for stronger tools, but no one had thought to bring any. One of the young men ran to a nearby house and borrowed an ax. 'Abdu'l-Bahá raised it high and cut through the earth. Meanwhile, another young man ran to the elevated train tracks and asked the workers to loan him a shovel, which he brought back to 'Abdu'l-Bahá.

'Abdu'l-Bahá asked a Bahá'í named Lua Getsinger to be the first person to scoop the earth from the site. She resisted until He called her a second time, then she came forward and did as He asked. Then Corinne True took a turn. After that, Bahá'ís from different countries each came forward to share in the occasion. Shovels of earth were overturned by people from many backgrounds: Persian, Syrian, Egyptian, Indian, North American Indian, Japanese, South African, English, French, German, Dutch, Norwegian, Swedish, Danish, and Jewish.

When the hole was fairly large, 'Abdu'l-Bahá reached down and picked up handfuls of dirt, which He shared with several people. Then He placed the stone, pushed the soil around it, and declared, "The Temple is already built."⁵

The next day, Corinne held a Bahá'í funeral for her son, Davis. 'Abdu'l-Bahá visited Davis's grave a few days later, and said prayers for him, as well as for Corinne's husband and other children buried nearby. He told Corinne that she would one day be together with her children again.

* * *

"Thousands of Mashriqu'l-Adhkárs . . . will be built in the East and in the West, but this, being the first one erected in the Occident, has great importance."

— *'Abdu'l-Bahá*

14

Shining Stars

"Whenever and wherever there were children, 'Abdu'l-Bahá would go to them and they would come to Him. . . . He was always prepared to meet and please His visitors, be they high or low, children or poor. And aside from being the treasure of knowledge and wisdom and the ocean of all things of the spirit, 'Abdu'l-Bahá always kept Himself well supplied with material things to bestow upon those who went to Him. Flowers, candy, money, clothing . . . these were for distribution among the friends and the needy and everybody else but Himself."[1]

Early in the morning on May 5, the Bahá'í children eagerly gathered in the parlor of the Plaza Hotel with their parents. When 'Abdu'l-Bahá came into the room, the children all began to sing for Him. He carried two baskets filled with flowers—one with roses and the other with carnations. The baskets also held sealed envelopes. The children were coming from all over Chicago, and none of the Bahá'ís had known how many would arrive.

'Abdu'l-Bahá called each child, and each one came up to greet Him. He whispered to them in English, asking their names, and they answered joyfully. 'Abdu'l-Bahá gave each child a rose, a carnation, and an envelope filled with rose petals. There were three roses, carnations, and envelopes left in the baskets after He had greeted each child. Then three more children rushed in. 'Abdu'l-Bahá hurried over to them and gave them the remaining gifts.

Then He spoke to them:

You are the children of whom Christ has said, "Of such is the kingdom of God"; and according to the words of Bahá'u'lláh you are the very lamps or candles of the world of humanity, for your hearts are exceedingly pure and your spirits most sensitive. . . . May you develop so that each one of you shall become imbued with all the virtues of the human world. May you advance in all material and spiritual degrees. May you become learned in sciences, acquire the arts and crafts, prove to be useful members of human society and assist the progress of human civilization. May you be a cause of the manifestation of divine bestowals—each one of you a shining star radiating the light of the oneness of humanity toward the horizons of the East and West. May you be devoted to the love and unity of mankind, and through your efforts may the reality deposited in the human heart find its divine expression. I pray for you, asking the assistance and confirmation of God in your behalf.

You are all my children, my spiritual children. Spiritual children are dearer than physical children, for it is possible for physical children to turn away from the Spirit of God, but you are spiritual children and, therefore, you are most beloved. I wish for you progress in every degree of development. May God assist you. May you be surrounded by the beneficent light of His countenance, and may you attain maturity under His nurture and protection. You are all blessed.[2]

'Abdu'l-Bahá then addressed the children's parents, and His words included this advice:

Be in perfect unity. Never become angry with one another. Let your eyes be directed toward the kingdom of truth and not toward the world of creation. Love the creatures for the sake of God and not for themselves. You will never become angry or impatient if you love them for the sake of God. Humanity is not perfect. There are imperfections in every human being, and you will always be unhappy if you look toward the people themselves. But if you look toward God, you will love them and be kind to them, for the world of God is the world of perfection and complete mercy. Therefore, do not look at the shortcomings of anybody; see with the sight of forgiveness. The imperfect eye beholds imperfections. The eye that covers faults looks toward the Creator of souls.[3]

'Abdu'l-Bahá walked slowly around the circle of children, touching each one's head in a loving blessing. Then He walked with the group to Lincoln Park, which stretched for several miles along the shore of Lake Michigan. Albert Kilius, a Bahá'í photographer who had traveled to Chicago from Spokane, Washington, was waiting to photograph 'Abdu'l-Bahá. Albert took several photographs, including one of 'Abdu'l-Bahá with a group of children and adults.

After they returned to Spokane, Albert and his wife, Annie, sent more than seven hundred photos to 'Abdu'l-Bahá. Albert continued to make copies of the photographs throughout his life. He never charged anyone for them, even when he had little money. In the years ahead, Annie corresponded with 'Abdu'l-Bahá and He encouraged her to share the Bahá'í Faith with others.

After leaving Chicago, 'Abdu'l-Bahá briefly visited Cleveland, Pittsburgh, and Washington, D.C. He had promised to attend a peace conference in New York, and as that date approached, His companion Maḥmúd said, "He moved like lightning from place to place. . . . In a very short time He accomplished many great tasks. Because the meetings in these cities had been scheduled in advance, several were held in one day and thousands of people were attracted and transformed by Him."[4]

When in Pittsburgh, many of the Bahá'ís asked 'Abdu'l-Bahá if He was pleased with His rooms at the hotel. To each He replied, "*Khaili khoob! Khaili khoob!*" ("Very good! Very good!") When His visitors had left, He turned to a Bahá'í named Dr. Zia Bagdadi and said with a smile, "The friends here are anxious to know if I like these rooms! They do not know what we had to go through in the past. Imagine the conditions and surroundings when we were exiled by the Turkish Government and were imprisoned in the barracks of 'Akká; Bahá'u'lláh occupied one room; His family and several other families were forced to occupy one room. Aside from the severe illness that was raging, and the death of many among us prisoners—adults and children—on account of unsanitary surroundings and starvation, I noticed that my own presence in that crowded room was another source of torture to all of them. This was due to the fact that parents and children were suppressing and restraining themselves by trying to be quiet and polite in my presence. So, in order to give them freedom, I accepted the morgue of the barracks, because that was the only room available, and I lived in it for about two years. Now the kind friends here wish to know if I like these magnificent rooms!"[5]

* * *

"You are all my children, my spiritual children."

—'Abdu'l-Bahá

15

A Treasured Gift

When 'Abdu'l-Bahá left Chicago, Dr. Zia Bagdadi joined Him, working as a writer and translator. Zia's father and grandfather had been involved in the earliest days of the Bahá'í Faith. When Zia was young, he often visited Bahá'u'lláh and 'Abdu'l-Bahá. Zia wrote about his treasured memories of being with Bahá'u'lláh at the Mansion of Bahjí near 'Akká, one of the two homes in which Bahá'u'lláh lived after being allowed to leave the city in 1877:

> I had the greatest honor and privilege to see Bahá'u'lláh and sit at his feet many days and nights in this palace. Here he used to hold my hand while walking to and fro in his large room, revealing Tablets, chanting the prayers with the most charming and melodious voice, while one of the attendants took them down. . . . On hot days he would take me with him to the outer alcove of the

palace where it was somewhat cooler. . . . the gentle breezes blew on his soft jet black hair which reached almost to the waist. . . .

At times he would spend half an hour on the alcove, and my eyes would remain fixed on his majestic face. But whenever he glanced at me with his brown, piercing, yet most affectionate eyes, then I had to turn mine away and look down on the floor.

At my birth, Bahá'u'lláh named me "Zia" (Light) and gave me the Turkish title, "Effendi." But on my first visit to him, when he inquired about my health, I replied in Arabic, "*Mabsoot*" (I am happy). He questioned, "How is your father?" "*Mabsoot*"; and "How is your mother?" "*Mabsoot*," was my reply. He laughed heartily and after that he always called me Mabsoot Effendi (The Happy One).[1]

When Zia grew up, he moved to Chicago. He completed his training as a medical doctor about a year before 'Abdu'l-Bahá came to the United States. He also wrote the Persian pages of the Bahá'í publication, *Star of the West*.

During 'Abdu'l-Bahá's visit, He, along with some other Bahá'ís, spent some time at the Lake Mohonk Mountain House. It was nestled among green valleys, wooded hills, and waterfalls, about four hours away from New York City. This was the site of a world-famous annual peace conference founded in 1895 by a Quaker man named Albert Smiley. Each year, about three hundred leaders in government, business, religion, the press, and education came from many countries to discuss the need for world peace. Hundreds of well-known leaders had attended the conferences, including William Howard Taft,

America's twenty-seventh president, and Andrew Carnegie, an influential businessman who gave most of his fortune to charity. Because of Mr. Smiley's peace work, he was nominated for the Nobel Peace Prize.

In 1912, our planet had not yet suffered a global war. But in northern Africa, a war was raging between Italy and Turkey. Mistrust and conflict grew throughout Europe. Several countries began to quickly increase their military supplies. The countries near the Balkan Mountains of southeastern Europe fought two wars between 1912-1913. All these events contributed to the start of World War I in 1914. Several times during His travels in North America, 'Abdu'l-Bahá spoke about unrest in Europe. He said, "A world-enkindling fire is astir in the Balkans. God has created men to love each other; but instead, they kill each other with cruelty and bloodshed."[2]

On May 14, 1912, 'Abdu'l-Bahá shared His hopeful vision of peace with the guests at Lake Mohonk. Mr. Smiley introduced 'Abdu'l-Bahá with the greatest praise and respect. 'Abdu'l-Bahá then spoke about universal peace and the oneness of humanity.

Maḥmúd wrote, "A new spirit and a new excitement seemed to prevail over the gathering. During the day most of the delegates had been engaged in materialistic issues. . . . In the evening, however, they found themselves puzzled when they heard the eloquent, elegant address of the Master concerning the unity of all people. . . ."[3]

After 'Abdu'l-Bahá spoke, the audience applauded enthusiastically. They asked Him to continue, but He was tired, so He kindly apologized. The participants came forward to shake His hand—some even embraced Him. Then Mr. Smiley's wife gave 'Abdu'l-Bahá a pendant that had been designed for the conference.

'Abdu'l-Bahá stayed at Lake Mohonk for three days. Many dignitaries visited with Him and were impressed with His dynamic, loving spirit. One sunny day while He was out walking, 'Abdu'l-Bahá met a group of young women and men. He stopped under a blossoming tree and smiled at them. Then He told them a story about some rats and mice that held a conference about how to make peace with the cat. After a long discussion, they decided that the best plan would be to tie a bell around the cat's neck. The rats and mice would then hear the cat approaching and would be able to get out of his way. But when they tried to decide who should have the dangerous job of hanging the bell on the cat, no one was brave enough to do it. The conference ended in confusion.

Everyone laughed at the story. Then 'Abdu'l-Bahá mentioned that the story was a lot like a global peace conference. There were many ideas and words, but no one wants to try to hang a bell on world leaders. At that, the group's faces grew more serious.

On His last evening at the conference, 'Abdu'l-Bahá said, "We have to leave this place tomorrow and I wish I had one of my Persian rugs here, that I might give it as a present to our host, Mr. Smiley. . . ."

It was already nine o'clock at night, and 'Abdu'l-Bahá was planning to depart at ten o'clock the next morning. His companions told Him that it would be impossible for anyone to travel to His apartment in New York and return with a rug in time. Then 'Abdu'l-Bahá turned to Zia Bagdadi and said, "Well, what do you say?"

Zia replied, "I am not afraid to try anything for you, my Lord."

Zia set off. He took a carriage from Lake Mohonk to the railroad station. There was no passenger train to New York at that time, but a freight train was just leaving. Zia jumped on the tracks and ran after the train as fast as he could. Finally, he was able to grab the caboose of the train and climb up. As he stood panting and catching his breath, the conductor came forward and ordered him to get off of the train.

Zia showed the conductor his business card and said he was on a very urgent mission. The conductor said, "O you are a doctor! That is all right." He didn't ask for details, so Zia didn't explain that his mission was to obtain a rug.

At about two o'clock in the morning, Zia reached 'Abdu'l-Bahá's apartment overlooking the Hudson River. He had to wake Grace Ober and her sister Ella Roberts, who were serving as housekeepers in the apartment. They were surprised to find Zia with no hat, his hair messy, and his clothes covered in dust. They kindly asked him to rest and have something to eat, but he told them he didn't have time. He selected one of 'Abdu'l-Bahá's most precious rugs and hurried back to the railway station.

Zia took the first train in the morning and reached the Lake Mohonk station at nine o'clock. He was still an hour away from the lake, and there was no vehicle in sight. Finally, the mail wagon appeared. When the mail-carrier went inside to collect the mail, Zia got onto the wagon and waited for him. The mail-carrier was surprised to find a passenger when he returned to finish his mail route.

Zia explained that he was in the service of 'Abdu'l-Bahá, and showed him the rug he had to deliver. Zia even offered to take over the job of driving the wagon and delivering the mail for that day. He was flooded with relief when the mail-carrier said, "It's alright I guess, I am going up there anyway."

The mail wagon arrived at Lake Mohonk just as 'Abdu'l-Bahá was shaking hands with Mr. Smiley and preparing to leave. Smiling, 'Abdu'l-Bahá took the rug from Zia, and presented it to Mr. Smiley.

"Why this is just what I have been seeking for many years!" exclaimed Mr. Smiley. "You see we had a Persian rug just like this one, but it was burned in a fire and ever since my wife has been broken-hearted over it. This will surely make her very happy."[4]

Mr. Smiley passed away in December of that year. His half-brother, Daniel Smiley, continued to host the peace conferences until 1916.

16

Wings of a Bird

In 1912, when 'Abdu'l-Bahá visited the United States, American women did not have the right to vote (also known as suffrage). Women had been working to gain suffrage and other basic rights for more than sixty years. The first women's rights meeting in this country was held in Seneca Falls, New York, in 1848. At that time, in addition to being unable to vote, women did not have the right to give public speeches, testify in court, control their own wages, own property, or have custody of their own children.

By 1912, women had earned these rights in some parts of the country. They could control their wages in two-thirds of the states. But those wages were very low, and were often earned in unsafe and difficult conditions. Women might work for eleven or twelve hours a day— sometimes seven days a week. Though it was illegal, girls as young as eight were hired, and hidden in crates during inspections. They worked in buildings that were poorly maintained and barely heated in winter.

If they spent an extra few minutes in the bathroom, it was deducted from their pay. They were not allowed to speak to each other during working hours. When women went on strike to try to obtain better conditions, some were arrested and even assaulted by the police.

Tragic attention was brought to women's working conditions in 1911 when 146 employees (mostly female European immigrants) died in a fire at a garment factory called the Triangle Shirtwaist Company in New York City. (A shirtwaist was a button-down blouse) The owners had locked the doors from the outside to prevent employees from leaving during working hours. The women were trapped in the building when the fire started, and there was no sprinkler system. Women clung to breaking fire escapes on the ninth floor, but fire fighters' ladders could only reach the sixth floor. Some women jumped from windows to their death. It took a week for family members to identify their loved ones, and seven women could not be identified at all. A funeral was held for the unnamed women, and a three-hour funeral procession marched through New York in the pouring rain.

Eight months later, the company owners were found not guilty of any wrongdoing. One juror at the trial stated that he thought the employees were "not as intelligent as those in other walks of life and were therefore more susceptible to panic." Two years later, one of the owners again locked his female employees in their workroom. He was fined just twenty dollars.[1]

Many women felt that until they could vote, they had no real chance of improving their lives. But not all women agreed. Some felt that participating in politics was unfeminine, and that their husbands or fathers represented them at the polls. Many anti-suffragists believed that giving women the right to vote would destroy the American way of life. They predicted that wives and husbands would argue over politics, and women would try to control their husbands at home.

Racism also influenced the suffrage movement. White women sometimes treated black suffragists unfairly. Some white women were willing to accept a law that gave only white women the right to vote, and excluded black women. White men, especially in the South, opposed rights for any blacks—including suffrage for black women. Others, in both the North and the South, supported suffrage for women as a way to limit the influence of blacks. They felt that white women voters would help them outnumber the total votes of black men and women.

Over the years, some states and western territories had granted women the right to vote, and at times, the right had been revoked. In 1912, women could vote in nine states—Wyoming, Colorado, Idaho, Utah, Washington, California, Arizona, Kansas, and Oregon.[2] But many suffragists still insisted on voting rights for all women in the United States.

'Abdu'l-Bahá had been asked for His opinion on suffrage by a reporter before He even reached the American shore. He replied,

The modern suffragette is fighting for what must be, and many of these are willing martyrs to imprisonment for their cause. . . .

The world in the past has been ruled by force, and man has dominated over woman by reason of his more forceful and aggressive qualities both of body and mind. But the scales are already shifting—force is losing its weight and mental alertness, intuition, and the spiritual qualities of love and service, in which woman is strong, are gaining ascendency. Hence the new age will be . . . an age in which the masculine and feminine elements of civilization will be more properly balanced.[3]

To draw attention to their cause, women began holding suffrage parades in New York City in 1910. From just 400 marchers in 1910, the parade had grown to include 20,000 marchers by May 6, 1912, while half a million people watched. Women marched in the ankle-length dresses and elaborate hats that were popular at the time. They held signs, wore sashes, and even carried umbrellas with slogans about women's suffrage. Some rode on horses or in automobiles; others walked with their children or pushed baby carriages.

At the time of the parade, 'Abdu'l-Bahá was in Cleveland, Ohio. But just two weeks later, on May 20, He addressed a group of suffragists in New York. When He entered, everyone stood up with excitement and happiness. Mrs. Penfield, the chairperson of the meeting, gave a warm introduction: "I have the great honor tonight to present to you one of the most distinguished advocates of both Women's Suffrage and Universal Peace. . . . I cannot use better language than that of one of his followers when I describe 'Abdul-Bahá in these words: 'Abdul-Bahá wishes to be known as 'The Servant of Humanity.' He seeks no higher station than this, yet when one understands all this means, one realizes the combination of humanity and exaltation which it implies."[4] 'Abdu'l-Bahá addressed the crowd:

In past ages it was held that woman and man were not equal—
that is to say, woman was considered inferior to man. . . . The
idea prevailed universally that it was not allowable for her to step
into the arena of important affairs. . . . She was denied the right
and privilege of education and left in her undeveloped state.
Naturally, she could not and did not advance. In reality, God
has created all mankind, and in the estimation of God there is no
distinction as to male and female. The one whose heart is pure is
acceptable in His sight, be that one man or woman. . . .

The most momentous question of this day is international peace
. . . and universal peace is impossible without universal suffrage.
Children are educated by the women. The mother bears the troubles
and anxieties of rearing the child, undergoes the ordeal of its birth
and training. Therefore, it is most difficult for mothers to send to
the battlefield those upon whom they have lavished such love and
care. . . . So it will come to pass that when women participate fully
and equally in the affairs of the world, when they enter confidently
and capably the great arena of laws and politics, war will cease; for
woman will be the obstacle and hindrance to it. . . .

The purpose, in brief, is this: that if woman be fully educated
and granted her rights, she will attain the capacity for wonderful
accomplishments and prove herself the equal of man. . . . Both
are human; both are endowed with potentialities of intelligence
and embody the virtues of humanity. In all human powers and
functions they are partners and coequals.[5]

According to Maḥmúd, after 'Abdu'l-Bahá spoke, "There was great excitement in the audience, and, as in other gatherings, the people were deeply moved and both men and women shook His hand, supplicating for assistance."[6]

'Abdu'l-Bahá spoke out in support of women's rights throughout His travels. He said, "The world of humanity is possessed of two wings: the male and the female. So long as these two wings are not equivalent in strength, the bird will not fly."[7]

Women continued working for suffrage throughout World War I, from 1914-1918. They also supported soldiers as nurses on the battlefield and as factory workers at home. This service may have helped men to see them as equals. In early 1919, President Woodrow Wilson spoke in favor of the 19th Amendment to the Constitution, which would allow women to vote. Finally, in August 1920, the amendment had been approved by 36 of the 48 states then in the union, and it became law. Women across the nation had earned their hard-won right to vote.

* * *

"In the estimation of God there is no distinction as to male and female. The one whose heart is pure is acceptable in His sight, be that one man or woman. . . . "

—*'Abdu'l-Bahá*

17

A Blessed Anniversary

During His travels in New York, some of the Bahá'ís planned a small celebration for 'Abdu'l-Bahá's birthday, which was on May 23. One day—though the exact date is not known—they baked a cake as a surprise, and took taxis to the Bronx. 'Abdu'l-Bahá was in the first taxi, and when they stopped at a park, He got out and walked ahead of the others.

A group of boys gathered around 'Abdu'l-Bahá and started to laugh at Him. Two or three of them threw stones. Some of the Bahá'ís were concerned and hurried to help Him, but He told them to stay away. 'Abdu'l-Bahá just smiled as the boys taunted Him and pulled at His clothing.

Then 'Abdu'l-Bahá turned to the Bahá'ís and said, "Bring me the cake."

They were shocked—no one had told Him about the cake. Some said, "But 'Abdu'l-Bahá, the cake is for your birthday."

He repeated, "Bring me the cake."

One friend brought out a large cake with white icing. The boys grew quiet and stared at it hungrily. 'Abdu'l-Bahá took the cake and looked at it with pleasure. Then He asked for a knife, which was also brought to Him. 'Abdu'l-Bahá counted the boys, then cut the cake into the same number of pieces. Each boy took a piece of cake, ate it, and then ran away, contented.[1]

On May 22, 'Abdu'l-Bahá traveled to Boston, Massachusetts. That evening, He spoke to nearly three thousand people—including many elected officials and eight hundred Christian ministers from Unitarian churches around the United States and Canada. 'Abdu'l-Bahá was introduced by the Lieutenant-Governor of Massachusetts, who said, "Tonight we express our highest respect and heartfelt gratitude in this great gathering for this highly revered and peace-loving personage who has come from the East to the West to promote the principles of the oneness of humanity and universal peace." The entire audience stood and gave Him a long ovation.[2]

On May 23, 'Abdu'l-Bahá traveled to Clark University in Worcester, Massachusetts. As He watched the green countryside during the fifty-mile trip from Boston, He said, "I wish that Bahá'u'lláh had come to these regions. So fond was He of such scenery that often while traveling, wherever the country was more beautiful and more verdant, He would ask His company to make a stop. Once while passing by the shore of a lake, the green country, the purity of the water and the beauty of the weather were so lovely in the eyes of Bahá'u'lláh that He asked that the caravan be stopped and all remained there for several hours."[3]

In the early evening, 'Abdu'l-Bahá arrived in Cambridge, a city near Boston, and went to the home of Alice and Francis Breed. The Breeds' daughter, Florence Khán, had held a special luncheon in 'Abdu'l-Bahá's honor in Washington, D.C., with her husband, 'Alí Kulí Khán. Alice and Francis Breed had traveled widely, and their luxurious home was filled with treasures from such places as Russia, Alaska, and China. Beautiful greenhouse flowers decorated the home, and the Bahá'í children had gathered wildflowers as well. Alice Breed baked a cake for 'Abdu'l-Bahá's visit—but her first cake fell, so she had to bake another.

May 23 is an important day in the history of the Bahá'í Faith. On that date in 1844, in Shíráz, Persia (now Iran), a young man known as the Báb ("the Gate" in Arabic) announced that a new Messenger of God would soon appear. The Báb Himself was also a Messenger of God. He devoted His life to preparing the world for the Prophet to follow—Bahá'u'lláh. Also on May 23, at midnight, 'Abdu'l-Bahá was born in Tehran, Persia.

Both the Báb and Bahá'u'lláh are revered in the Bahá'í Faith. They are the only two Messengers of God known to have lived on Earth at the same time. The Bahá'í calendar begins in 1844, the year of the Báb's announcement.

On that May evening in Cambridge, in addition to remembering the Báb, the Bahá'ís wanted to celebrate 'Abdu'l-Bahá's birthday. 'Abdu'l-Bahá graciously accepted their kindness. But He felt that the Báb's Declaration was much more important than His own birth. He spoke to the group about the importance of that event:

This is 23 May, the anniversary of the message and Declaration of the Báb. . . . On this day in 1844 the Báb was sent forth heralding and proclaiming the Kingdom of God, announcing the glad tidings of the coming of Bahá'u'lláh and withstanding the opposition of the whole Persian nation. Some of the Persians followed Him. For this they suffered the most grievous difficulties and severe ordeals. . . . They sacrificed their lives most willingly and remained unshaken in their faith to the very end. Those wonderful souls are the lamps of God, the stars of sanctity shining gloriously from the eternal horizon of the will of God.

The Báb was subjected to bitter persecution in S̲h̲íráz, where He first proclaimed His mission and message. A period of famine afflicted that region, and the Báb journeyed to Iṣfahán. There the learned men rose against Him in great hostility. He was arrested and sent to Tabríz. From thence He was transferred to Mákú and finally imprisoned in the strong castle of C̲h̲ihríq. Afterward He was martyred in Tabríz. . . .

He withstood all persecutions and bore every suffering and ordeal with unflinching strength. The more His enemies endeavored to extinguish that flame, the brighter it became. Day by day His Cause spread and strengthened. During the time when He was among the people He was constantly heralding the coming of Bahá'u'lláh. . . .

The Báb has admonished us . . . to be completely attracted by the love of Bahá'u'lláh, to love all humanity for His sake, to be lenient and merciful to all for Him and to upbuild the oneness of the world of humanity. Therefore, this day, 23 May, is the anniversary of a blessed event.[4]

After 'Abdu'l-Bahá's talk, Alice brought out the cake. It was decorated with sixty-eight candles, for 'Abdu'l-Bahá's age, and tiny flags from the United States, Iran, and England. She asked 'Abdu'l-Bahá to light the first candle, then each person took a turn lighting a candle. Maḥmúd wrote, "Mrs. Breed, indeed, lit the candle of servitude and steadfastness that evening, and in doing so, became the recipient of bounty from 'Abdu'l-Bahá's presence."[5]

'Abdu'l-Bahá kindly allowed Alice Breed to serve the cake on this occasion, but He did not want the Bahá'ís to celebrate His birthday. Instead, He said the day should only be associated with the Báb. Since the Bahá'ís wanted to have a day on which they could celebrate 'Abdu'l-Bahá, He gave them November 26, which became known as the Day of the Covenant.

A few days later, on May 26, Florence had her own birthday. She visited 'Abdu'l-Bahá at His hotel with her father, Francis. Florence noticed that her father seemed worried. She told him, "There is nothing to be afraid of. 'Abdu'l-Bahá is very kind. He is always friendly and considerate."

"I'm not afraid, but I don't know what to say to Him," her father answered.

"Oh, you can at least thank Him for His great kindness to me, during my visit to Him in 1906."

"Oh yes! Yes indeed. I can do that." Francis seemed relieved.

When they arrived in 'Abdu'l-Bahá's room, a Persian interpreter was there to help them. 'Abdu'l-Bahá asked how they were and asked about their family. Then Francis said, "I want to thank you, 'Abdu'l-Bahá, for your hospitality and your many great kindnesses to my daughter when she went to Persia."

'Abdu'l-Bahá seemed moved. "Why do you thank me?" He said. "You are my own family."

When they left, He filled Florence's arms with white roses.[6]

18

The Portrait

When Juliet Thompson was ten years old, she dreamed of someday painting Jesus Christ. She even began to pray about it. She felt that the portraits she had seen didn't do Him justice—she wanted to paint Him as the "King of Men." When she grew up, she still hoped to do this—until she met 'Abdu'l-Bahá. That was when, she said, "I knew that no one could paint the Christ. Could the sun with the whole universe full of its radiations, or endless flashes of lightning be captured in paint?"

On the night before He arrived in New York, 'Abdu'l-Bahá sent a Tablet to one of Juliet's friends, saying, "On My arrival in America Miss Juliet Thompson shall paint a wonderful portrait of Me."

When Juliet heard this news, she was flooded with emotion: "surprise and dismay, fear, joy and gratitude all mixed together."[1]

Later, 'Abdu'l-Bahá asked Juliet, "Can you paint Me in a half hour?"

"A half hour . . . ?" she stammered. She had never finished a portrait in less than two weeks.

He said, "Well, I will give you three half hours. You mustn't waste My time, Juliet."

Juliet began the portrait early on a Saturday morning in June. She had decided to use pastels—powdered colors shaped into sticks. 'Abdu'l-Bahá sat in a small, cramped space with little light. Juliet liked to work while standing, but there was only room for her to sit. She said, "I found myself faced with every kind of handicap."

Then 'Abdu'l-Bahá said, "I want you to paint My *Servitude* to God."

Juliet was in a panic. She cried, "Only the Holy Spirit could paint *Your* Servitude to God. No human hand could do it. Pray for me, or I am lost. I implore You, inspire me."

"I will pray," He answered, "and as you are doing this only for the sake of God, you will be inspired."

And then, Juliet said, "An amazing thing happened. All fear fell away from me and it was as though Someone Else saw through my eyes, worked through my hand.

"All the points, all the planes in that matchless Face were so clear to me that my hand couldn't put them down quickly enough, couldn't keep pace with the clarity of my vision. I painted in ecstasy, free as I had never been before."[2]

Juliet found that this special inspiration continued each time she worked on the portrait. She wrote, "Oh, these sittings: so wonderful, yet so humanly difficult! We move from room to room, from one kind of light to another. The Master has given me three half hours, each time in a different room, and each time people come in and watch me. But the miraculous thing is that nothing makes any difference. The minute I begin to work the same rapture takes possession of me. Someone Else looks through my eyes and sees clearly; Someone Else works through my hand with a sort of furious precision."[3]

One day, Juliet brought her pastels when she visited 'Abdu'l-Bahá. She had thought He might pose for her, but she found Him looking tired. He smiled at Juliet and asked her what she wanted.

She hid her paints and said, "Only to be near You."

"You must excuse Me from sitting for you today. I am not able today."

Later that day, 'Abdu'l-Bahá went for a walk. As Juliet was walking to the bus station, she passed 'Abdu'l-Bahá on His walk. He stopped her, took her hand, and smiled "with indescribable tenderness." He said, "Come tomorrow and paint, Juliet."

He looked a bit refreshed, but Juliet was still worried about Him. She wanted to answer in one of the few Persian statements she knew, just to amuse Him. She meant to say, "If Your health is good." But instead she said, *"Agar Shumá khúb ast,"* or "If You are good."

In her diary, Juliet wrote, "I was covered with confusion. I *must* have amused Him!"[4]

'Abdu'l-Bahá actually posed for Juliet six times, but she had completed the portrait in three half hours. At one sitting, another artist came in with a drawing she had done from a photograph. She asked 'Abdu'l-Bahá if she could add some touches from life, so He had to change His pose.

At the fourth sitting, Juliet began to paint while her friend Lua Getsinger sat on a couch nearby. Lua could speak Persian, and 'Abdu'l-Bahá said to her in Persian, "This makes me sleepy. What shall I do?"

Juliet said, "Tell the Master, Lua, that if He would like to take a nap, I can work while He sleeps."

Juliet wrote, "But I found that I could not. What I saw then was too sacred, too formidable. He sat still as a statue, His eyes closed, infinite peace on that chiseled face, a God-like calm and grandeur in His erect head."[5]

The sixth time 'Abdu'l-Bahá posed for Juliet, she wrote, "I didn't put on a single stroke. I was looking at the portrait wondering what I could find to do, when He suddenly rose from His chair and said: 'It is finished.'"[6]

The completed portrait was exhibited by Juliet's friend, Reverend Percy Grant, in the chapel of his parish house. In November, when 'Abdu'l-Bahá wished to take the portrait back with Him to Haifa, Juliet wrote to Percy, "I want to thank you too for your hospitality to the Master's picture. . . . You have given to many an opportunity to see at least a portrayal, if a very weak one, of a dear face which I doubt if most of us will see again."[7]

Juliet also sold photographs of the portrait, and she planned to give the money she earned from them to help fund the Bahá'í Temple. On the day before 'Abdu'l-Bahá left the United States, He took Juliet's hand and said, "I know your circumstances, Juliet. You have not complained to Me, you have said nothing, but I know them. I know your affairs are in confusion, that you have debts, that you have that house, that you have to take care of your mother. Now I want you to keep the money for yourself. . . . Do not feel unhappy . . . this is best."[8]

A pastel painting has a distinctive appearance, but its surface is delicate. It must be carefully preserved in order to avoid smudging and damage from light, humidity, and other factors. A friend of Juliet's wrote that the portrait was "time-damaged, it had to be restored, and Juliet felt the original was gone forever."[9] But perhaps just as treasured as the image Juliet created of 'Abdu'l-Bahá is her heartfelt diary, where she records their many conversations during her 1909 pilgrimage, His 1911 travels in Europe, and His time in the New York area. On His last day in the United States, 'Abdu'l-Bahá told Juliet, "Remember, I am with you always. Bahá'u'lláh will be with you always."[10]

19

Roses of God's Garden

On June 16, 'Abdu'l-Bahá spoke at the Fourth Unitarian Church in Brooklyn, New York. When 'Abdu'l-Bahá arrived, the pastor greeted Him with reverence and escorted Him up to the pulpit. After 'Abdu'l-Bahá spoke to the congregation about unity, the pastor invited Him to speak to the children's Sunday school. The children sang for Him, and then He spoke to them:

> I am glad to see these bright, radiant children. God willing, all of them may realize the hopes and aspirations of their parents.
>
> Praise be to God! I see before me these beautiful children of the Kingdom. Their hearts are pure, their faces are shining. They shall soon become the sons and daughters of the Kingdom. Thanks be to God! They are seeking to acquire virtues and will be the cause of the attainment of the excellences of humanity. This is the cause of oneness in the Kingdom of God. Praise be to God! They have

kind and revered teachers who train and educate them well and who long for confirmation in order that, God willing, like tender plants in the garden of God they may be refreshed by the downpour of the clouds of mercy, grow and become verdant. In the utmost perfection and delicacy may they at last bring forth fruit.

I supplicate God that these children may be reared under His protection and that they may be nourished by His favor and grace until all, like beautiful flowers in the garden of human hopes and aspirations, shall blossom and become redolent of fragrance.

O God! Educate these children. These children are the plants of Thine orchard, the flowers of Thy meadow, the roses of Thy garden. Let Thy rain fall upon them; let the Sun of Reality shine upon them with Thy love. Let Thy breeze refresh them in order that they may be trained, grow and develop, and appear in the utmost beauty. Thou art the Giver. Thou art the Compassionate.[1]

The prayer that 'Abdu'l-Bahá revealed is one that is often said by Bahá'í children.

* * *

"O God! Educate these children. These children are the plants of Thine orchard, the flowers of Thy meadow, the roses of Thy garden. Let Thy rain fall upon them; let the Sun of Reality shine upon them with Thy love. Let Thy breeze refresh them in order that they may be trained, grow and develop, and appear in the utmost beauty. Thou art the Giver. Thou art the Compassionate."

—'Abdu'l-Bahá

20

Creating a Precious Relic

Soon after 'Abdu'l-Bahá came to New York, He was asked to appear in a motion picture. He answered, "*Khaili Khub*" ("Very good").[1]

Movies were still a fairly new invention at that time. The earliest films were viewed by just one person at a time with a Kinetoscope. This device was developed in 1891 by William Kennedy Laurie Dickson, an assistant of the inventor Thomas Edison. The film was enclosed in a wooden cabinet about four feet high, and the viewer looked through an opening at the top.

A few years later, projectors were made to show movies to larger audiences in Europe and the United States. The films lasted just fifteen to ninety seconds, offering short glimpses of everyday life and real events, as well as acted scenes. Then longer films became popular, including comedies and adventures. The films were silent, though entertainers often performed along with them, adding narration, sound effects, and music. Later, sound was recorded on large disks to be played with the movies. By around 1930, movie studios recorded sound directly onto film.

On June 18, 'Abdu'l-Bahá went to the MacNutt home in Brooklyn to be filmed by Howard MacNutt and J.G. Grundy. Howard and Mary MacNutt became Bahá'ís in 1898. When they visited 'Abdu'l-Bahá in 'Akká in 1905, Howard said to 'Abdu'l-Bahá, "I wish it were possible for me to take thy living face back to New York that the believers there might see as I see."

'Abdu'l-Bahá answered, "My love is my face; take it to them; tell them to see me in their love for each other."[2]

Howard and J.G. Grundy made the film. The first scene shows 'Abdu'l-Bahá riding in a car and then being greeted by the Bahá'ís. Then He is shown walking and speaking to the Bahá'ís:

Observe the power of the Ancient Beauty and the influence of the Greatest Name through which He has united us with the people of America in this way. If all the powers of the world had joined forces, still it would have been impossible that hearts could be attracted to such a degree and that we should be assembled in a meeting such as this with so much love, loving one another heart and soul. See what the power of Bahá'u'lláh has done! He has made the people of the East and of the West love one another. But for His power, the holding of such an assembly would have been impossible. Praise be to God that we are united and that we are of one heart and soul.[3]

In one scene of the film, 'Abdu'l-Bahá is seated with children all around Him. In another scene of the film, 'Abdu'l-Bahá says good-bye to the Bahá'ís, and encourages them to be happy, saying:

Rejoice! Rejoice! The Sun of Reality has dawned.

Rejoice! Rejoice! The New Jerusalem has descended from heaven.

Rejoice! Rejoice! The glad tidings of God have been revealed.

Rejoice! Rejoice! The mysteries of the Holy Books have been fulfilled.

Rejoice! Rejoice! The Great Day has come.

Rejoice! Rejoice! The banner of the oneness of humanity is hoisted.

Rejoice! Rejoice! The tent of universal peace is pitched.

Rejoice! Rejoice! The Divine Lamp is illumined.

Rejoice! Rejoice! The breezes of the Merciful are wafting.

Rejoice! Rejoice! The joyful tidings and promises of the Prophets have come to pass.

Rejoice! Rejoice! The Glory of Carmel has shed its effulgence on the world.

Rejoice! Rejoice! The East and the West have embraced.

Rejoice! Rejoice! America and Asia like unto two lovers have joined hands.[4]

Howard and J.G. Grundy wrote an article about the film, saying, "all these were never-to-be-forgotten scenes, but those who beheld his countenance in the final utterance of the 'Glad-Tidings' will treasure the memory of it forever."[5]

'Abdu'l-Bahá also agreed to have His voice recorded on what was known as the "Edison talking machine," so His voice could be heard along with the motion picture. Using this device, sound was recorded on a cylinder made of a wax-like material. The article stated, "Consider what this means! The beloved friends one hundred years from now will be able to see the form, face, and actions" of 'Abdu'l-Bahá, "and even more, listen to the actual tone of his voice speaking the words which the pictures so eloquently portray."[6]

Later that summer, the film was shown in Chicago, New York, and Muskegon, Michigan.

The National Spiritual Assembly of the Bahá'ís of the United States calls the film "one of the most sacred and precious relics associated with the life and ministry of 'Abdu'l-Bahá." The Assembly states that "the film must be handled with great dignity and that showings must be very occasional." The Assembly also shares guidance from the Universal House of Justice, the international governing body of the Bahá'í Faith, stating that "this rare archival treasure" will be shown "in an atmosphere of the utmost reverence and sanctity." The House of Justice will decide on appropriate times to show the film.[7]

In addition to filming 'Abdu'l-Bahá, Howard MacNutt took notes during at least eighteen of 'Abdu'l-Bahá's talks. Later, Howard collected as many of 'Abdu'l-Bahá's talks as he could find, and prepared them to be published. 'Abdu'l-Bahá approved the project and said the book should be called *The Promulgation of Universal Peace*. 'Abdu'l-Bahá told Howard, "This service . . . shall make thee the object of the praise and gratitude of the friends in the East as well as the West."[8]

21

City of the Covenant

One afternoon, Juliet Thompson was working on 'Abdu'l-Bahá's portrait at His rented house in New York, while her friend Lua Getsinger sat nearby. 'Abdu'l-Bahá took a brief nap. Then, Juliet wrote, "Suddenly, with a great flash like lightning He opened His eyes and the room seemed to rock like a ship in a storm with the Power released. The Master was *blazing.*"

Lua and Juliet were moved to tears. Then 'Abdu'l-Bahá spoke to Lua. Juliet heard the words, "Herald of the Covenant," in Arabic.

Shocked, Lua exclaimed in Persian, "I?"

'Abdu'l-Bahá said, "Call one of the Persians. You must understand this."

Juliet wrote, "Never shall I forget that moment, the flashing eyes of 'Abdu'l-Bahá, the reverberations of His Voice, the Power that still rocked the room."

'Abdu'l-Bahá told her, through an interpreter, "I appoint you, Lua, the Herald of the Covenant. And I AM THE COVENANT, appointed by Bahá'u'lláh. And no one can refute His Word. This is the Testament of Bahá'u'lláh. You will find it in the Holy Book of Aqdas.[1] Go forth and proclaim, 'This is THE COVENANT OF GOD in your midst.'"

"A great joy had lifted Lua up. Her eyes were full of light. She looked like a winged angel. 'Oh recreate me,' she cried, 'that I may do this work for Thee!'"

Then, suddenly, the moment had passed. Juliet wrote, "He sat before us now in His dear humanity: very, very human, very simple."[2]

What did 'Abdu'l-Bahá mean by "the Covenant"? A covenant is an agreement. Each Messenger of God makes a Covenant with His followers. The Messenger gives people His teachings and guidance, and in return, they agree to follow His laws.

The Bahá'í Faith is unique in the history of religions because Bahá'u'lláh left His followers written instructions about who would lead the Bahá'í Faith after His passing. Bahá'u'lláh appointed 'Abdu'l-Bahá as the leader of the Bahá'ís and the only person authorized to interpret Bahá'u'lláh's teachings. 'Abdu'l-Bahá is called the "Center of the Covenant." This protects the Bahá'í Faith from breaking apart into different groups.

That afternoon, 'Abdu'l-Bahá sent Lua to "proclaim" the Covenant to the guests who were waiting for Him. She prepared them for His talk that would follow. This wasn't the first time He had given Lua a special task.

When Lua met 'Abdu'l-Bahá in late 1898, she was an actress and singer of twenty-seven. She and her husband Edward were part of the very first group of westerners to visit 'Abdu'l-Bahá in 'Akká. On the first day, 'Abdu'l-Bahá told Lua, "The love of God burning in your heart is manifest upon your face and it gives us joy to look upon you."[3]

The Getsingers returned to visit 'Abdu'l-Bahá in 1900 and 1901. Each time, they listened carefully to His teachings, took notes, and shared them with the Bahá'ís in America. At home, they received many letters from 'Abdu'l-Bahá, and they made copies of them so others could read His words.

In the fall of 1902, Lua was in Paris, France, at 'Abdu'l-Bahá's request. 'Abdu'l-Bahá had asked Lua to take a petition to the <u>sh</u>áh of Persia (now Iran), requesting his help to protect the Bahá'ís in that country. From the early days of the Bahá'í Faith, religious and government leaders in Iran often arrested, imprisoned, and even killed Bahá'ís because of their beliefs.

Visiting the highest ruler of a country is not an easy task. Lua prayed constantly that she would succeed in reaching the <u>sh</u>áh and persuading him to help the Bahá'ís. Along with a French Bahá'í named Hippolyte Dreyfus, Lua went to the hotel where the <u>sh</u>áh was staying. The <u>sh</u>áh's advisor promised that every effort would be made to grant her petition. But Lua insisted on seeing the <u>sh</u>áh for herself. She entered the reception hall where 150 Persian men were waiting for a chance to meet with the <u>sh</u>áh. The only woman in the room, she bravely stepped forward and handed her petition to him. The <u>sh</u>áh promised to do all in his power to satisfy her request.

'Abdu'l-Bahá praised Lua's efforts, writing, "O maid-servant of God! I was informed of that which thou has accomplished in Paris & the people of Sanctity are therefore praising thee. Verily, I will not forget this, & beg of God to increase thy faith, assurance, firmness, steadfastness, love & attraction."[4]

Sadly, violent persecution continued, and a second petition signed by Lua and other Bahá'ís was sent to the sháh in Iran the following year. The persecutions did ease for a time. However, oppression of Bahá'ís intensified at different periods, and it continues to this day.

Over the years, Lua visited 'Abdu'l-Bahá at least eight times. At one point she spent more than a year living in His household and teaching English to His family. She found it heartbreaking to leave Him. One Bahá'í friend who joined her on a trip to 'Akká wrote, "I shall never forget how Lua Getsinger sobbed as if her heart would break as she slowly descended the long flight of steps, looking back frequently at 'Abdu'l-Bahá who stood benignly at the top. And I shall never forget how joyously 'Abdu'l-Bahá smiled at Lua's tears, knowing that they were more precious than pure gold. . . . the instinctive expression of her great love."[5]

Lua served the Bahá'í Faith passionately, and the intensity of her faith impressed others. While in 'Akká, she was often asked to speak with people who were unfamiliar with the Faith or opposed to it, and she was able to move them deeply. Her faith was a comfort to 'Abdu'l-Bahá as well. He would sometimes ask her to sing the hymn "Nearer, My God, to Thee," and her clear, sweet voice brought tears to His eyes. He even kept a small, framed portrait of Lua in one of the rooms at Bahjí, where the Shrine of Bahá'u'lláh is located.

Not all of the tasks 'Abdu'l-Bahá gave to Lua were as momentous as visiting the sháh. One day, 'Abdu'l-Bahá told her He was too busy to visit a friend who was sick. He asked Lua to go in His place, and to bring food to the man and care for him. Lua agreed immediately. She was pleased to be able to help 'Abdu'l-Bahá.

But she swiftly returned and exclaimed, "Master, surely you cannot realize to what a terrible place you sent me. I almost fainted from the awful stench, the filthy rooms, the degrading condition of that man and his house. I fled lest I contract some terrible disease."[5]

'Abdu'l-Bahá looked at her sadly and said that if she wanted to serve God, she must serve other people. He told her to go back to the man's house. If it was dirty, she should clean it. If the man was hungry, she should feed him. 'Abdu'l-Bahá had done this many times—could Lua not do this once? Lua understood the example He was calling her to follow, and she did as He asked. Afterward she often volunteered to nurse people who were ill or wounded.

When she was in the United States, Lua spent almost all of her time giving talks and classes about the Bahá'í Faith. 'Abdu'l-Bahá sent her and Edward many letters of encouragement. In 1911, 'Abdu'l-Bahá asked her to go to California to teach. She stayed for about a year, even spending some time in Mexico, and spoke to large numbers of people. Then Lua traveled to Chicago to attend 'Abdu'l-Bahá's dedication of the cornerstone for the Bahá'í House of Worship.[7]

From then on, Lua spent every moment she could in His presence. It was June 19 when 'Abdu'l-Bahá asked Lua to "proclaim" the Covenant to 125 people who were waiting for Him to speak. On that day, He named New York City the "City of the Covenant."

'Abdu'l-Bahá at one point explained His own station as the Center of the Covenant:

Today, the most important affair is firmness in The Covenant, because firmness in The Covenant wards off differences.

In former cycles no distinct Covenant was made in writing by the Supreme Pen; no distinct personage was appointed to be the Standard differentiating falsehood from truth. . . .

But in this Dispensation of the Blessed Beauty (BAHA'O'LLAH) among its distinctions is that He did not leave people in perplexity. He entered into a Covenant and Testament with the people. He appointed a CENTER OF THE COVENANT. He wrote with His own pen. . . . Whatsoever his (Abdul-Baha's) tongue utters, whatsoever his pen records, that is correct; according to the explicit text of BAHA'O'LLAH in the Tablet of THE BRANCH. . . .

This is the Covenant which BAHA'O'LLAH made. If a person shall deviate, he is not acceptable at the Threshold of BAHA'O'LLAH. In case of difference, Abdul-Baha must be consulted."[8]

'Abdu'l-Bahá asked Lua to return to California, but she couldn't bear to be separated from Him. At that time, it looked as though 'Abdu'l-Bahá would not be traveling to California. When the Bahá'ís were gathered for an outdoor meeting, Lua went out into the woods and deliberately walked back and forth in poison ivy. When her feet were completely poisoned, she said to her friend Juliet Thompson, "Now, Julie, He *can't* send me to California."

Early the next morning, 'Abdu'l-Bahá, sent Juliet to visit Lua, who was staying at a hotel.

Lua was in bed, her feet horribly swollen. "*Look* at me, Julie," she said. "*Look* at my feet. Oh, please go right back to the Master and tell Him about them and say: 'How can Lua travel now?'"

Juliet did as she asked. 'Abdu'l-Bahá laughed, then walked across the room to a bowl of fruit and selected an apple and a pomegranate.

"Take these to Lua," He said. "Tell her to eat them and she will be cured. Spend the day with her, Juliet."

Juliet wrote, "Oh precious Lua—strange mixture of disobedience and obedience—and all from love! I shall never forget her, seizing first the apple, then the pomegranate and gravely chewing them all the way through till not even a pomegranate seed was left: thoroughly eating her cure, which was certain to send her to California."

Late that afternoon, Juliet wrote, when 'Abdu'l-Bahá visited Lua, her feet were "beautifully slim" once again.[9]

22

Unity Feast

On June 20, 'Abdu'l-Bahá said, "It is my wish to give a large feast of unity. A place for it has not yet been found. It must be outdoors under the trees, in some location away from city noise—like a Persian garden. . . . All the friends will come. They will be my guests. . . . Each will be as a leaf, blossom or fruit upon one tree. For the sake of fellowship and unity I desire this feast and spiritual gathering."[1]

The site that 'Abdu'l-Bahá chose for the unity feast was the home of Roy Wilhelm in West Englewood (now Teaneck), New Jersey. In a letter, 'Abdu'l-Bahá later wrote to Roy, "I am extremely pleased with you because you are a true Bahá'í. Your house is My house; there is no difference whatsoever between yours and Mine."[2]

In 1900, when he was about twenty-five years old, Roy had begun attending Bahá'í meetings in New York with his parents. His mother, Laurie, had a strong interest in religion and investigated various beliefs.

After learning about the Bahá'í Faith, Laurie soon began exchanging letters with Bahá'ís around the world.

In 1907, Roy and Laurie visited 'Abdu'l-Bahá in 'Akká. Roy went to the Shrine of the Báb on Mount Carmel in Haifa to take some photographs. He found several Persians sitting around a table there. They didn't speak English, but Roy showed them his camera, and they understood that he wanted to take pictures. Then he saw a Bahá'í ring on the finger of one of the men who was closest to him. Roy whispered, "Alláh-u-Abhá," which means "God the All-Glorious" in Arabic, and is used as a greeting among Bahá'ís.

"Alláh-u-Abhá!" the man answered immediately. He then jumped up and hugged Roy, kissing him on both cheeks. Then the whole group crowded around Roy, and as he later wrote, "I knew that I was among friends."[3]

While Roy and Laurie were in 'Akká, 'Abdu'l-Bahá said to them, "You represent all the American believers. In you I see all the American believers. Your faces are shining. I have been waiting long for your coming. Thank God that you came."

They answered, "We do thank God and hope to become more worthy."

He answered, "You will become more worthy."[4]

During his stay, Roy's room was near a garden where 'Abdu'l-Bahá would sit in a tent and meet with visitors. Roy noticed that people of all faiths, including businessmen, government officials, and religious leaders, came to 'Abdu'l-Bahá for advice and guidance.

Roy also saw that every Friday about one hundred of 'Akká's poorest people came to see 'Abdu'l-Bahá. Roy wrote, "He will be seen to give to each a small coin, and to add a word of sympathy or cheer; often an inquiry about those at home; frequently He sends a share to an absent one. . . . They all look forward to this weekly visit, and indeed it is said that this is the chief means of sustenance for some of them. Almost any morning, early, He may be seen making the round of the city, calling upon the feeble and the sick; many dingy abodes are brightened by His presence."[5]

The Wilhelms's home in West Englewood had a large wooded grove with evergreen trees, and it was there that the Bahá'ís gathered for 'Abdu'l-Bahá's Feast. Tables were set out in a circle under the trees.

Maḥmúd wrote, "The green lawn under the shade trees was strewn with flowers so that it seemed as if an embroidered carpet had been spread. . . . To see the Master walking in this green, flower-covered garden, with a gentle breeze blowing, the purity of the air, the cleanliness of the surroundings and the rejoicing of the friends, was most pleasing; all seemed to vie with one another to please the Master."[6]

One of the Bahá'ís who attended was Juliet Thompson, who came with a friend. Juliet wrote, "We walked from the little station, past the grove where the tables were set—a grove of tall pine trees—and on to the house in which *He* was, He Whose Presence filled our eyes with light and without Whom our days had been very dim and lifeless.

"Ah, there He was again! Sitting in a corner of the porch! I sped across the lawn . . . forgetting everything. He looked down at me with grave eyes, and I saw a fathomless welcome in them."[7]

When everyone had gathered, 'Abdu'l-Bahá spoke to the group:

This is a delightful gathering; you have come here with sincere intentions, and the purpose of all present is the attainment of the

virtues of God. The motive is attraction to the divine Kingdom.
Since the desire of all is unity and agreement, it is certain that this
meeting will be productive of great results. . . . Like candles these
souls will become ignited and made radiant through the lights
of supreme guidance. Such gatherings as this have no equal or
likeness in the world of mankind. . . .

May you become as the waves of one sea, stars of the same
heaven, fruits adorning the same tree, roses of one garden in order that through you the oneness of humanity may establish its
temple in the world of mankind, for you are the ones who are
called to uplift the cause of unity among the nations of the earth.

First, you must become united and agreed among yourselves.
You must be exceedingly kind and loving toward each other. . . .
Your utmost desire must be to confer happiness upon each other.
Each one must be the servant of the others, thoughtful of their
comfort and welfare. In the path of God one must forget himself entirely. He must not consider his own pleasure but seek the
pleasure of others. He must not desire glory nor gifts of bounty
for himself but seek these gifts and blessings for his brothers and
sisters. It is my hope that you may become like this, that you may
attain to the supreme bestowal and be imbued with such spiritual
qualities. . . .[8]

'Abdu'l-Bahá provided the Persian food for dinner, along with
sherbet and many sweets. When dinner was ready and everyone was
seated, 'Abdu'l-Bahá anointed each person with attar of rose. "He
spoke to them in a voice that was sweeter than honey. . . . the

surroundings were green and verdant with trees in full bloom perfuming the air."⁹

Juliet Thompson wrote:

> To me the most beautiful scene of all came later, when the Master returned to us after dark. . . . All over the lawn, on each side of the path, sat the others, the light summer skirts of the women spread out on the grass, tapers in their hands (to keep off mosquitoes). In the dark, in their filmy dresses, they looked like great moths and the burning tips of the tapers they waved like fireflies darting about.
>
> Then the Master spoke again to us. I was standing behind Him, close to Him, and before He began He turned and gave me a long, profound look. . . .
>
> Before He had finished He rose from His chair and started down the path still talking, passing between the dim figures on the grass with their lighted tapers, talking till He reached the road, where He turned and we could no longer see Him. Even then His words floated back to us. . . .
>
> "Peace be with you," this was the last we heard, "I will pray for you."
>
> Oh that Voice that came back *out of His invisibility* when He had passed beyond our sight. May I always remember, and *hear the Voice*.¹⁰

As 'Abdu'l-Bahá walked among the Bahá'ís in the moonlit evening, a carriage passed by. The riders saw 'Abdu'l-Bahá, stopped the carriage, and joined the group to listen.

On another visit to the Wilhelm home, 'Abdu'l-Bahá joined the Wilhelms for dinner at the nearby home of Louis Bourgeois. Louis was a French-Canadian architect who would later design the Bahá'í House of Worship in Wilmette, Illinois.

The following year, the Bahá'ís commemorated 'Abdu'l-Bahá's unity feast with another gathering. Roy received a letter from 'Abdu'l-Bahá saying, "That annual memorial meeting will be the souvenir of Abdul-Baha, especially when it is passed with infinite delight and gladness."[11]

Today the location of this beautiful event is known as the Wilhelm Bahá'í Properties. On the grounds stands a log cabin that Roy built with the help of architect Louis Bourgeois. The study of rocks and stones was Roy's hobby, and he brought stones for his fireplace from around the world. In front of the cabin is a rock garden with pools of water, fountains, and colored lights. Bahá'ís in the area gather regularly for devotions, music, and Bahá'í classes. And each year, a unity feast is held in June, to commemorate 'Abdu'l-Bahá's warm and welcoming unity feast.

* * *

"May you become as the waves of one sea, stars of the same heaven, fruits adorning the same tree, roses of one garden in order that through you the oneness of humanity may establish its temple in the world of mankind. . . ."

— 'Abdu'l-Bahá

23

Bahá'í Marriage

On July 17, Grace Robarts and Harlan Ober stood together in a large, beautiful room in a New York home. Just the day before, 'Abdu'l-Bahá had suggested that they get married. They were probably close friends, and they were happy that He had encouraged their marriage, so they agreed.

Throughout 'Abdu'l-Bahá's journey in America, Grace worked as a housekeeper in whatever home He was staying. He chose her to go ahead to the next city and find an apartment for Him, and have it ready for His arrival. Then she "kept the home immaculate, and always ready for the constant stream of guests from morning to night, Bahá'ís and inquirers and souls in difficulty to whom 'Abdu'l-Bahá was always a loving Father."[1] She made each temporary home attractive and welcoming. 'Abdu'l-Bahá later wrote, "During our stay in America, Mrs. Ober served with heart and soul."[2]

Grace Robarts was born in Canada, and her father was an Anglican clergyman. As a child, she told her mother that she felt she had a gift to share with the world. She often went with her father on visits to help the people in his parish. When she grew up, she became a teacher of household arts at a college in Canada.

A friend wrote about Grace, "She was unique in that there was no such word as 'stranger' in her vocabulary. She was, to an amazing degree, a friend to all the world. Wherever she was, in a public conveyance, in a public gathering, at a summer resort—people were just people—her people, and she held out the hand of friendship to them. . . . She seemed unconscious of anything but the highest in each soul."[3]

Harlan, who had been born in Massachusetts, was a lawyer. He had a deep interest in religion from childhood, when he went to Sunday school and to prayer meetings in neighbors' homes. When he grew up, he attended a Bahá'í class taught by Lua Getsinger. She said, "You must discover the reality of this Faith and, if it is true, you must accept it, but if it is false, you must denounce it."[4] She encouraged him to pray.

In the spring of 1906, Harlan rented a hotel room in Boston and went there to pray and study the Bible and the Bahá'í writings. After a while, feeling confused, he said a prayer to God through Jesus, asking for understanding. Harlan said:

Through the mercy and bounty of God, doors opened, knowledge replaced uncertainty and ignorance. . . . When I went out into the streets and through the Boston Common and the Boston Public Gardens, I looked upon every soul . . . with a new love. I saw in the blossoming of the magnolias the clear evidence of the return of spirit as outlined in the writings of Bahá'u'lláh. . . . [5]

That November, 'Abdu'l-Bahá asked a Bahá'í named Hooper Harris to go to India to teach the Bahá'í Faith. Lua suggested that Harlan go along. On their way to India, they stopped in 'Akká to visit 'Abdu'l-Bahá. He invited them to a Feast with forty Persian friends. Harlan said:

> 'Abdu'l-Bahá went around the long table, heaping high each plate. Then when all were served He walked back and forth, the lights showing on His face and flowing robe, and gave a talk. . . . The large room, the long table, the varied Oriental costumes, the wonderful faces of the believers, the spirit that was present as everyone turned to 'Abdu'l-Bahá etched an unforgettable picture on our hearts.[6]

Later, He gave them guidance about teaching in India:

> In India people believe that God is like the sea and man is like a drop in the sea, or that God is like the warp and man is like the woof of this coat. But the Bahá'ís believe that God is like the sun and man is like a mirror facing the sun. . . .
> Whenever difficult questions or problems come to you, turn your hearts to the heart of 'Abdu'l-Bahá and you will receive help.[7]

During the seven months that Hooper and Harlan traveled in India, they relied on 'Abdu'l-Bahá's instructions. When they turned their hearts to Him, every question was answered. Later 'Abdu'l-Bahá wrote that Harlan "rendered a great service to the Kingdom of God" with this trip.[8]

On Harlan and Grace's wedding day, 'Abdu'l-Bahá led the simple Bahá'í ceremony in the morning. The Bahá'í marriage ceremony requires only that in the presence of two witnesses, the couple each say, "We will all, verily, abide by the Will of God."

Since Bahá'í marriage ceremonies were not considered official in the United States at that time, a regular, civil ceremony was also necessary. Howard Colby Ives, who was a Unitarian minister and not yet a Bahá'í, performed this ceremony in the evening. Today, Bahá'í marriage ceremonies are legal in the United States. They are overseen by an elected administrative body called a Local Spiritual Assembly, which approves the witnesses and ensures that all other requirements are met.

Juliet Thompson wrote that Grace and Harlan were "transfigured; they seemed to be bathed in white light."[9] Friends from different races and different parts of the world, including Europe, Iran, Russia, India, and what is now Israel, all gathered to celebrate with them. One wrote, "Never before in America had such a wedding as this been witnessed. All seemed to feel the Power of the Holy Spirit."[10]

After the civil ceremony, 'Abdu'l-Bahá stood up. He wore a cream-colored cloak and fez (brimless hat), and His long white hair fell almost to His shoulders. As the bride and groom kneeled, He raised His hands, palm upwards, level with His waist, and chanted a prayer for them:

Glory be unto Thee, O my God! Verily, this Thy servant and this Thy maidservant have gathered under the shadow of Thy mercy and they are united through Thy favor and generosity. O Lord! Assist them in this Thy world and Thy kingdom and destine for them every good through Thy bounty and grace. O Lord! Confirm them in Thy servitude and assist them in Thy service. Suffer them to become the signs of Thy Name in Thy world and protect them through Thy bestowals which are inexhaustible in this world and the world to come. O Lord! They are supplicating the kingdom of Thy mercifulness and invoking the realm of Thy singleness. Verily, they are married in obedience to Thy command. Cause them to become the signs of harmony and unity until the end of time. Verily, Thou art the Omnipotent, the Omnipresent and the Almighty![11]

Then 'Abdu'l-Bahá said, "This is a blessed evening."[12]

The following morning, 'Abdu'l-Bahá said, "The holding of last night's meeting was done with wisdom and it produced great love. The marriage of the Bahá'ís was also performed according to Christian rites, so that the world may know that the people of Bahá are not confined by trivial customs, that they respect all nations and their peoples, that they are free from all prejudices and associate with all religions with utmost peace and happiness."[13]

Several years after their marriage, the Obers adopted three children—one English, one German, and one Russian. They spent their summers on a farm at what is now Green Acre Bahá'í School, in Maine. Many people said they found "deep spiritual sustenance" there. Grace used her gifts to make her home restful and cheerful. It was described as "a home for the soul as well as for the body." Everyone who visited was welcomed by Grace "with radiant cheer and enthusiasm. Each one felt that he or she had come to his home of dreams where love dwelt continually and warmed the heart, and each one was made to feel that it was *his* home—the home of love and unity. The secret of the remarkable atmosphere lay in the fact that she considered her home not as hers but the home of 'Abdu'l-Bahá."[14]

In 1916, the Obers received a letter from 'Abdu'l-Bahá:

O ye two firm ones in the Covenant!

Although we are living in the holy land and you are dwelling in the United States, yet the spiritual relations and the communication of the hearts are firm and steadfast because the unity of the Divine Essence has bonded us together. In this material world we are cemented together and, God willing, in the Universe of God, the world of the Kingdom, we will be the associates and intimates of each other. . . . Upon ye be greeting and praise![15]

In addition to the Obers, another Bahá'í couple was married during 'Abdu'l-Bahá's visit to America. Although 'Abdu'l-Bahá was not present at their wedding, He had also encouraged them to marry, just He had done with Harlan and Grace. In September, Louisa Mathew and Louis Gregory united in the first marriage between a black and white Bahá'í.

Louisa Mathew had learned about the Bahá'í Faith in Paris, France, while she was studying music. She had grown up in a wealthy family in England. Although it was unusual for girls to attend college, her parents sent her to Cambridge University, where she studied economics, languages, and music. She had a beautiful soprano voice, and later continued her studies in Paris.

After she became a Bahá'í, Louisa wrote to 'Abdu'l-Bahá and asked for permission to visit Him. At that time, He was in Egypt. 'Abdu'l-Bahá invited her to come. Her trip had to be delayed several times, but she was finally able to go to Egypt. While there, she met Louis Gregory, an African American Bahá'í who was visiting from America. After her pilgrimage, Louisa returned to Paris.

When 'Abdu'l-Bahá came to America, Louisa joined Him. She boarded His ship, the S.S. *Cedric,* when it stopped in Naples, Italy. While on the ship, 'Abdu'l-Bahá mentioned that He would be happy if she would marry Louis.

'Abdu'l-Bahá had said, "Intermarriage is a good way to efface racial differences."[16] He also wrote to a Washington, D.C., Bahá'í, "If it be possible, gather together these two races, black and white, into one assembly and put such love into their hearts that they shall not only unite but even intermarry."[17]

However, interracial marriage was not accepted in the United States at that time. Scientists said that mixing the races was harmful. Interracial marriage was actually illegal or not recognized in twenty-five states—including all of the South. Louis and Louisa were both mature people who were fond of each other. Their friendship grew into love. They bravely decided to follow 'Abdu'l-Bahá's advice.

Because interracial marriage was controversial, the wedding was simple and quiet. It was held in New York, on September 27, with only a few friends present.

Because of the racist attitudes of the time, Louis and Louisa faced constant disapproval and the threat of violence. It was difficult for them to travel together—or even find a place to live. They often traveled separately, each serving the Bahá'í Faith. Still, their marriage was happy. Louis wrote after one summer together in New Hampshire, "I was greatly blessed . . . by . . . the presence of my angel wife. . . . We were supremely happy together in our quaint old home near the sea."[18]

'Abdu'l-Bahá wrote to them, "Continually do I remember you. I beg of God that through you good fellow-ship may be obtained between the white and the black for you are an introduction to the accomplishment."[19]

24

A Delightful Spot

From Portsmouth, New Hampshire, Sarah Farmer eagerly waited for 'Abdu'l-Bahá to visit her. She was about sixty-five years old and in poor health. She wrote to 'Alí Kulí <u>Kh</u>án, in Washington, D.C., about her excitement to see 'Abdu'l-Bahá: "He is so gentle and loving that we have only to see Him to love Him. . . . For twelve years I have looked forward toward welcoming [H]im to Green Acre. . . . If I were on my feet I would soon be where He is. The longing to see Him is beyond all description."[1]

Green Acre was Sarah Farmer's gift to the world. It began as the Eliot Hotel, which Sarah opened with four business partners in 1890. But soon Sarah was inspired with a unique vision. She saw Green Acre as a peaceful retreat where people could learn about different religions and ideas. She said, "How much more good would come from a summer vacation if instead of being burdened with the effort of finding amusement for leisure hours, one's mind and soul could be refreshed by helpful thoughts, under spreading pines, in green pastures, beside still waters."[2]

In 1894, Sarah started the Green Acre Conferences. They began with the raising of the world's first known peace flag—a tradition that continues today. Green Acre attracted speakers from various religions, as well as writers, artists, teachers, and leaders in a variety of fields. Programs covered a wide range of topics, including peace, education, religion, art, music, psychology, nature, and many other subjects. Sarah encouraged guests to listen to them all with an open mind. She believed that all the world's Prophets had brought a message of peace to humanity.

In a few years, Green Acre was known worldwide. There were so many guests that they filled the inn, and more stayed in tents on the grounds. An article in *New England Magazine* declared, "The most distinctive feature of Green Acre is its noble persistency . . . to reveal the real unity of religious ideals despite their varying forms of expression. . . ."[3]

The Green Acre program for 1899 included a quotation from Bahá'u'lláh. The next year, Sarah visited 'Abdu'l-Bahá in 'Akká. She had a list of questions she wanted to ask Him, but somehow she left them in her room when she went to see Him. Without being asked, 'Abdu'l-Bahá answered every one of them.

After Sarah met 'Abdu'l-Bahá, the Bahá'í teachings were included in many of Green Acre's programs. Sarah felt that the Bahá'í Faith fulfilled her goals for Green Acre. She also said the Faith brought her "a joy greater than I have hitherto known."[4]

However, some people disagreed with this direction for Green Acre. Some even stole equipment from the school, to try to stop it from operating. Sarah faced financial problems. Her health suffered.

Over the years, 'Abdu'l-Bahá sent Sarah at least twenty-eight letters of encouragement. He wrote, "Thou art always in my memory and before my eyes. . . . I am assured that thou shall be enabled to render great services."[5]

A group called the Green Acre Fellowship was established to help organize the school. After a bad fall in 1907, Sarah's health declined. A few years later, friends placed her in a private clinic in Portsmouth.

When 'Abdu'l-Bahá reached Green Acre on August 16, 1912, more than five hundred people were waiting for Him. The road to the main inn was lined with multicolored lanterns. After giving a talk, He said, "I desire to offer a prayer in behalf of Miss Farmer; for, verily, she has been the founder of this organization, the source of this loving fellowship and assemblage." His prayer included these words:

> O Thou kind Lord! Bestow quick recovery through Thy power and bounty upon the founder of this Association. O Lord! This woman has served Thee, has turned her face toward Thy King-dom and has established these conferences in order that reality might be investigated and the light of reality shine.
>
> O Lord! Be Thou ever her support. O Lord! Be Thou ever her comforter. O Lord! Bestow upon her quick healing. Verily, Thou art the Clement. Verily, Thou art the Merciful. Verily, Thou art the Generous.[6]

'Abdu'l-Bahá stayed at Green Acre for a week, and He gave several talks during that time. He praised the beautiful location of Green Acre, as in this talk on August 17:

Are you all well and happy? This is a delightful spot; the scenery is beautiful, and an atmosphere of spirituality haloes everything. In the future, God willing, Green Acre shall become a great center, the cause of the unity of the world of humanity, the cause of uniting hearts and binding together the East and the West. This is my hope.

Tonight I wish to speak upon the oneness of the world of humanity. This is one of the important subjects of the present period. If the oneness of the human world were established . . . The people of the world would live together in harmony, and their well-being would be assured. . . .

When the light of Bahá'u'lláh dawned from the East . . . He said, "Ye are all the fruits of one tree, the leaves of one branch." . . .

Bahá'u'lláh has made no exception to this rule. . . . God is the Father of all. He educates, provides for and loves all; for they are His servants and His creation. . . . No matter to what religion a man belongs, even though he be an atheist or materialist, nevertheless, God nurtures him, bestows His kindness and sheds upon him His light. . . . Just as God loves all and is kind to all, so must we really love and be kind to everybody. . . . We must consider everyone as related to us, for all are the servants of one God. . . .

Everything must be done in order that humanity may live under the shadow of God in the utmost security, enjoying happiness in its highest degree.[7]

'Abdu'l-Bahá went to visit Sarah Farmer in Portsmouth. They drove back to Green Acre together. 'Abdu'l-Bahá described to her His vision for the future of Green Acre. He said, "This is hallowed ground made so by your vision and sacrifice. Always remember this is hallowed ground which I am pointing out to you."

'Abdu'l-Bahá walked around the grounds with Sarah, pointing out certain areas and speaking to her. He showed her where a Bahá'í university would someday be built. At another spot, He said, "This is where the second Bahá'í Temple in the United States will be raised. In reality, all this has been built and is right now ready to become a material reality whenever the Supreme Concourse finds mankind purified enough to bring about its consummation." He told Sarah, "You will be revered above all American women one fine day, you will see."[8]

One evening, He said, "My thoughts are wholly absorbed by this journey. I can think of nothing else because the outcome of this journey is so great. Up to now in the Cause of the Blessed Beauty a development as great as this has not occurred."[9]

One day a young girl came to 'Abdu'l-Bahá and said, "I have come to ask for your assistance. Please tell me what I am fitted to do so that I may occupy myself with it."

He asked, "Do you have trust in me?"

She said, "Yes."

He said to her, "Be a perfect Bahá'í. Associate with Bahá'ís. Study the teachings of Bahá'u'lláh. Then you will be assisted in whatever you undertake to do."

She said, "I am a good Jewess."

'Abdu'l-Bahá told her, "A good Jew can also become a Bahá'í. The truth of the religion of Moses and of Bahá'u'lláh is one. Turn toward

Bahá'u'lláh and you will acquire peace and tranquillity, you will hear the melody of the Kingdom, you will stir people's souls and you will attain the highest degree of perfection. Be assured of this."

She was so impressed with His words that she threw herself at His feet and wept.[10]

As He prepared to leave on August 23, 'Abdu'l-Bahá said, "We have finished our work here. We have sown a seed. Many souls have been attracted and transformed. Every day we have seen gifts such as fruit, flowers, honey and sweets which have been placed here anonymously and without show. This is a proof of the sincerity of their hearts."[11]

* * *

"Just as God loves all and is kind to all, so must we really love and be kind to everybody. . . . We must consider everyone as related to us, for all are the servants of one God."

— *'Abdu'l-Bahá*

25

Fred's Ride

Fred Mortensen's heart was beating fast as he walked onto the grounds of Green Acre. He was dirty, covered from head to toe with soot, and exhausted from his long journey. Fred had traveled from Cleveland, Ohio, to Eliot, Maine, by train—but not sitting comfortably in a seat. He couldn't afford a ticket, so he "rode the rods."

In the early 1900s, it was common for homeless or unemployed men to travel illegally on trains. They might jump in an empty boxcar, ride on top of the train, between the cars, on a ladder, or under the train, on boards stretched across the metal rods. This was, of course, very dangerous. Sharp curves, harsh weather, and other hazards led to many injuries and deaths. Also, railroad crewmen might deal violently with trespassers, or have them arrested.

At twenty-five years old, Fred already had a long history of trouble and difficulty. As a youth, he and his friends often drank alcohol, fought, stole, and destroyed others' property. Fred landed in jail, but managed to escape while awaiting trial. For the next four years, he was a fugitive. Then, as he tried to help a friend who was being arrested, some detectives noticed him. Later, Fred wrote, "in my haste to get away from them I leaped over a thirty-five foot wall, breaking my leg, to escape the bullets whizzing around about. . . ."[1]

The lawyer who defended Fred was a Bahá'í named Alfred Hall. In addition to handling the case, Alfred taught Fred about the Bahá'í Faith. Fred said he owed Albert "many thanks and my everlasting good will for helping to free me from the prison of men and of self. . . . It was he who told me, hour after hour, about the great love of 'Abdu'l-Bahá for all his children and that he was here to help us show that love for our fellowmen. . . . Thus the Word of God gave me a new birth, made me a living soul, a revivified spirit. I am positive that nothing else upon earth could have changed my character as mine has been changed."[2]

When Fred heard that 'Abdu'l-Bahá was at Green Acre and might not travel west again, he immediately decided he *must* visit Him. He left Minneapolis for a printers' convention in Cleveland, but he was too excited to stay for the entire meeting. The night before he left Cleveland, he dreamed that he was 'Abdu'l-Bahá's guest at a long table with many others, as 'Abdu'l-Bahá paced and told stories, gesturing with His hand. When Fred finally met 'Abdu'l-Bahá, he wrote, "he looked just as I saw him in Cleveland."[3]

After surviving his 700-mile trip, Fred arrived at Green Acre on the evening of August 20. Early the next morning, he joined a group in the main hall waiting to meet 'Abdu'l-Bahá. When 'Abdu'l-Bahá came in,

He paid little attention to Fred. Fred felt unhappy and thought to himself glumly, "It must be that He knows I stole a ride."[4]

But shortly after 'Abdu'l-Bahá left the room, one of His companions returned and said, "'Abdu'l-Bahá wishes to see Mr. Mortensen."

Fred later wrote, "Why, I nearly wilted. I wasn't ready. I hadn't expected to be called until the very last thing. I had to go, and it was with a strange feeling in my heart and wondering, wondering what would happen next."

But 'Abdu'l-Bahá welcomed him with a warm smile and a hand-clasp, and told him to be seated. 'Abdu'l-Bahá said, "Welcome! Welcome! You are very welcome."

'Abdu'l-Bahá asked, "Are you happy?" He repeated the question three times. Fred wondered why he asked so often. Of course I am happy, he thought.

Then 'Abdu'l-Bahá asked, "Did you have a pleasant journey?"

That was the question Fred had most wanted to avoid! He looked at the floor. But 'Abdu'l-Bahá asked him again, "Did you have a pleasant journey?"

Fred looked up and saw that 'Abdu'l-Bahá's eyes were like "sparkling jewels, which seemed to look into my very depths. I knew he knew and I must tell. . . ."

Fred said, "I did not come as people generally do, who come to see you."

"How did you come?"

"Riding under and on top of the railway trains."

'Abdu'l-Bahá said, "Explain how."

Fred looked again into the eyes of 'Abdu'l-Bahá. He wrote that "a wondrous light seemed to pour out. It was the light of love and I felt relieved and very much happier."

Fred explained how he rode on the trains. Then 'Abdu'l-Bahá kissed his cheeks, gave him some fruit, and even kissed the hat that had become filthy on the long trip.

When 'Abdu'l-Bahá was ready to leave Green Acre, Fred stood nearby. To his astonishment, 'Abdu'l-Bahá invited him to join His party. He took Fred to Malden, Massachusetts, as His guest for a week. Then He gave Fred enough money to return home comfortably. Fred wrote, "I left for home with never-to-be forgotten memories. . . . These events are engraved upon the tablet of my heart and I love every moment of them."[5]

About a year later, 'Abdu'l-Bahá wrote to Fred, "That trip of thine from Minneapolis to Green Acre will never be forgotten. Its mention will be recorded eternally in books and works of history. Therefore, be thou happy that, praise be to God, thou hast an illumined heart, a living spirit, and art vivified with merciful breath."[6]

26

In Montreal

May Maxwell made extensive preparations for 'Abdu'l-Bahá's visit to her lovely home on Mount Royal in Montreal, Canada. Long before He had arrived in New York, His visit had been publicized in the *Montreal Daily Star*. A newspaper article later invited people to telephone the Maxwell home at "Uptown 3015" to make an appointment to see Him. May and her husband Sutherland bought new furniture, and they offered Him the top three stories of their four-story house.

On the evening of 'Abdu'l-Bahá's arrival, Sutherland met Him at the train station with two carriages to take Him to the Maxwell home. A group of friends and the editor of the *Montreal Daily Star* were waiting to see Him. May told Him, "So many people have telephoned and sent letters about your arrival and I have replied to all. I have become very tired but I consider this fatigue the greatest comfort of my life."[1]

May had been interested in religion since childhood, though her family was not religious. She grew up in New Jersey, and she liked to go into the woods alone to pray. When she was eleven years old, she dreamed of a light so bright that she was actually blinded for a day. Years later, she dreamed of a man in Eastern clothing, beckoning to her from across the Mediterranean Sea.

As a young woman, she lived in Paris with her mother, grandmother, and brother for several years, while her brother studied architecture. She spoke French fluently. But May often suffered from poor health, though doctors did not know why.

A friend of May's family, Phoebe Hearst, was among the first group of Bahá'ís traveling to 'Akká in 1898, along with Lua and Edward Getsinger. May was twenty-nine years old, and had been bedridden for nearly two years. Phoebe asked Edward, a physician, to examine May. When he did, he suggested that his wife Lua had just what May needed. Lua visited May and told her, "There is a prisoner in 'Akká who holds the key to peace."

May cried out, "I believe! I believe!" Then she fainted.[2]

When she awoke, she told Lua about her dream of the Eastern man. Lua said, "This is 'Abdu'l-Bahá."[3]

In spite of her illness, May decided to join the trip to 'Akká. She kept a journal of her experiences. She said that when she met 'Abdu'l-Bahá, she felt overwhelmed by His pure and holy spirit.

'Abdu'l-Bahá invited His visitors to meet Him one Sunday morning under the cedar trees on Mount Carmel, where He had often sat with Bahá'u'lláh. But May grew ill the next day. She wrote about 'Abdu'l-Bahá's response:

He came directly to my room and walking over to my bedside took both my hands in His, passed His hand over my brow, and gazed upon me with such gentleness and mercy that I forgot everything but the love and goodness of God, and my whole soul was healed and comforted. I looked up into His face and said, "I am well now. . . ." But He smiled and shook His head and bade me remain there quietly, until He should return at noon. Although I had been suffering during the night, all pain and distress were gone. . . . On Sunday morning we awakened with the joy and hope of the meeting on Mount Carmel. The Master arrived quite early and after looking at me, touching my head and counting my pulse, still holding my hand He said to the believers present, "There will be no meeting on Mount Carmel to-day. . . . We could not go and leave one of the beloved of God alone and sick. We could none of us be happy unless all the beloved were happy.[4]

May and her friends were surprised that the plans were cancelled because of just one person. It was so different from their everyday world, where schedules were given more importance than people's emotions. She felt that 'Abdu'l-Bahá was showing them a different world where love guided everyone's actions.

When it was time for the group to leave 'Akká, 'Abdu'l-Bahá left them with encouraging words:

Now the time is come when we must part, but the separation is only of our bodies, in spirit we are united. . . . Never forget this:

look at one another with the eye of perfection; look at Me, follow Me, be as I am; take no thought for yourselves or your lives, whether ye eat or whether ye sleep, whether ye are comfortable, whether ye are well or ill, whether ye are with friends or foes, whether ye receive praise or blame; for all of these things ye must not care at all. . . . Behold a candle. . . . It weeps its life away drop by drop in order to give forth its flame of light.[5]

When May returned to Paris, she was the only Bahá'í in Europe. But she began to share her experiences and beliefs with others. She taught the Faith to many, including Hippolyte Dreyfus, the first French Bahá'í; Thomas Breakwell, the first English Bahá'í; and Juliet Thompson, who became her dear friend. Years later, May's daughter said, "I don't think I ever knew anyone who inspired the love Mother did. . . ." Another time she said, "I can truly say of her that I never knew anyone to cross her path whom she did not in some way benefit— and that is saying a lot."[6]

It was in Paris that May met William Sutherland Maxwell, her brother's best friend and a fellow student of architecture. Everyone called him William, but May called him Sutherland. They fell in love. But Sutherland was so shy that he had trouble expressing himself when he wanted to ask May to marry him. She finally said, "Sutherland, are you proposing to me?"

He said, "Yes."

May said, "I accept."[7] They were married in London in 1902.

May and Sutherland moved to Montreal, Canada, where he joined his brother Edward's architecture firm. Their talents blended well, and their firm became the largest in Canada until World War I. Their work included the Church of the Messiah in Montreal and the Montreal Museum of Fine Arts, along with many other important buildings.

Sutherland had an exceptional ability for fine drawing and design, and he designed the Maxwell home himself. He excelled at artistic details, and he liked to be involved in every aspect of his designs. He would sometimes take the chisel from the stone carver and make changes that he called "sweetening the lines." The craftsmen who worked with him had deep respect for his talent.

Sutherland was passionate about art and architecture of every culture and time period. He loved to collect books, and eventually had about four thousand volumes in his library. He also met with other architects and artists on Saturdays to paint. His watercolors were included in shows of the Royal Canadian Academy of Arts.

Today the work of Sutherland and Edward is considered a treasured contribution to the nation of Canada. The library at McGill University in Montreal includes 16,000 architectural drawings and 700 photographs of their work.

Sutherland was not at all interested in the Bahá'í Faith in the early days of his marriage. He told May, "You have become a Bahá'í. Very well, you are responsible for this yourself. I have no hand in it."[8] But he later became a Bahá'í. His faith deepened significantly when he joined his wife on a visit to 'Abdu'l-Bahá in 1909. In later years, Sutherland moved to Haifa and designed the arcade and superstructure for the Shrine of the Báb, one of the holiest Bahá'í shrines in the world.

On 'Abdu'l-Bahá's first day in Montreal, a reporter asked Him if He had a message for the people of Canada. 'Abdu'l-Bahá said, "Your country is very prosperous and very delightful in every aspect; you have peace and security amidst you; happiness and composure are your friends; surely you must thank God that you are so submerged in the sea of His mercy."[9]

The next afternoon, Sutherland invited 'Abdu'l-Bahá to take a carriage ride around Montreal. When they reached the huge Notre Dame church, 'Abdu'l-Bahá got out of the carriage and went inside. He gazed at the vast building, with its grand architectural details and exquisite sculptures. When the church opened in 1829, it was the largest house of worship in North America. It is an honored part of Montreal's heritage, and was named a basilica by the pope in 1982. 'Abdu'l-Bahá told His companions, "Behold what eleven disciples of Christ have accomplished, how they sacrificed themselves! I exhort you to walk in their footsteps. When a person is detached, he is capable of revolutionizing the whole world."[10]

On September 1, 'Abdu'l-Bahá spoke at the Unitarian Church of the Messiah, which had been designed by the Maxwell brothers. When He arrived at the church, the pastor met Him at the entrance and respectfully took His arm and walked with Him to the pulpit, where he offered 'Abdu'l-Bahá his own chair. After the service opened with music, the pastor read from the book of Isaiah in the Bible about the Promised One appearing in the East. Then the pastor introduced 'Abdu'l-Bahá, saying that His message was "the Message of God" and that "His presence in this church is the cause of eternal honor and the fulfillment of our long-cherished hopes and desires. . . . We extend

Him a sincere welcome and offer the incense of gratitude for His teachings which are the cause of the recovery of hearts and are the source of eternal blessings and happiness."[11] Then 'Abdu'l-Bahá spoke to the congregation:

> God, the Almighty, has created all mankind from the dust of earth. He has fashioned them all from the same elements; they are descended from the same race and live upon the same globe. . . . With impartial love and wisdom He has sent forth His Prophets and divine teachings. . . .
>
> Consequently, Bahá'u'lláh proclaimed that . . . the religion or guidance of God must be the means of love and fellowship in the world. If religion proves to be the source of hatred, enmity and contention, if it becomes the cause of warfare and strife and influences men to kill each other, its absence is preferable. . . .
>
> I pray God that these western peoples may become the means of establishing international peace and spreading the oneness of the world of humanity. . . .
>
> O Thou compassionate, almighty One! This assemblage of souls have turned their faces unto Thee in supplication. With the utmost humility and submission they look toward Thy Kingdom and beg Thee for pardon and forgiveness. O God! Endear this assembly to Thyself. Sanctify these souls, and cast upon them the rays of Thy guidance. Illumine their hearts, and gladden their spirits with Thy glad tidings. Receive all of them in Thy holy Kingdom; confer upon them Thine inexhaustible bounty; make them happy in this world and in the world to come. . . . O Lord! Make us brethren in Thy love,

and cause us to be loving toward all Thy children. Confirm us in service to the world of humanity so that we may become the servants of Thy servants, that we may love all Thy creatures and become compassionate to all Thy people. O Lord, Thou art the Almighty. Thou art the Merciful. Thou art the Forgiver. Thou art the Omnipotent.[12]

* * *

"O Lord! Make us brethren in Thy love, and cause us to be loving toward all Thy children. Confirm us in service to the world of humanity so that we may become the servants of Thy servants, that we may love all Thy creatures and become compassionate to all Thy people."

— 'Abdu'l-Bahá

27

A Home Becomes a Shrine

Many people heard about 'Abdu'l-Bahá's talk at the Church of the Messiah in Montreal, and they were eager to meet Him. A crowd gathered at the Maxwell home that evening. 'Abdu'l-Bahá spoke with so much energy and intensity that His *taj* (tall, brimless hat) fell from His head. Still, He continued to speak with vigor for more than half an hour:

> The people of this continent possess great capacity; they are the cause of my happiness, and I ever pray that God may confirm and assist them to progress. . . . No matter how much man may acquire material virtues, he will not be able to realize and express the highest possibilities of life without spiritual graces. . . .

Jesus Christ said, "Except a man be born of water and of the Spirit, he cannot enter into the kingdom of God.". . . . Before his first or physical birth man . . . had no knowledge of this world; his eyes could not see; his ears could not hear. When he was born . . . he beheld another world. The sun was shining with its splendors . . . the seas surging, trees verdant and green, all kinds of creatures enjoying life here. . . . For the perfect man there are two kinds of birth: the first, physical birth, is from the matrix of the mother; the second, or spiritual birth, is from the world of nature. . . . freedom from attachment to this mortal and material life. This is the second, or spiritual, birth of which Jesus Christ spoke in the Gospels. . . .

When a divine spiritual illumination becomes manifest in the world of humanity. . . . the banner of international peace will be upraised. . . . All humanity will appear as the members of one family. . . . The lights of the love of God will shine; eternal happiness will be unveiled; everlasting joy and spiritual delight will be attained.[1]

After His talk, 'Abdu'l-Bahá left the group and went to His room. But the people longed to hear more. Kindly, He came out and spoke to them again, explaining the immortality of the human spirit. Then some people asked to meet with Him individually in His room.

'Abdu'l-Bahá gave several public talks in Montreal and addressed more gatherings at the Maxwell home. He had planned to stay in Canada for only a few days, but He lengthened His visit to more than a week. During that time, thirty-four articles written about Him appeared in the Montreal daily newspapers. One day He remarked, "The value and greatness of these travels are not known now but will be apparent later on. As we had no other intention except to offer devotion to the Threshold of the One True God, we were assisted and the brightness of divine favor and grace appeared."[2]

One afternoon, 'Abdu'l-Bahá encouraged everyone to join Him for a Persian lunch cooked by one of His companions. He told this story:

To be grateful for the blessings of God in time of want and trouble is necessary. In the abundance of blessings everyone can be grateful. It is said that Sulṭán Maḥmúd cut a melon and gave a portion of it to Ayáz who ate it cheerfully and expressed gratitude. When the Sulṭán ate a little of the same melon, he found it bitter. He asked, "How did you eat such a bitter melon and show no sign of disliking it?" Ayáz answered, "I had eaten many sweet and palatable things from the hands of the Sulṭán and I thought it very unworthy of me to express dislike on eating a slightly bitter thing today." Thus man, who is immersed in the blessings of God, should not be grieved if he experiences a little trouble. He should not forget the manifold divine bounties.[3]

'Abdu'l-Bahá moved from the Maxwell home to the Hotel Windsor. The Maxwells tried to convince Him to stay, but He said, "A traveler should stay in a hotel." Perhaps He did not want to burden the household, because He was very careful about His personal expenses. Once when Maḥmúd asked if he should call a carriage, 'Abdu'l-Bahá preferred to take the streetcar, saying, "This saves expense. There is a difference of one dollar in the fare." Yet He was generous with others. He gave each of the Maxwells' servants one British pound.[4]

One afternoon, 'Abdu'l-Bahá and His companions took a car ride to the foot of Mount Royal, outside the city limits. This was a popular place for recreation. They traveled to the top in the "Mountain Elevator"—steam-powered cable cars that offered an alternative to the winding roads, footpaths, or wooden staircase. The ride cost five cents for adults and three cents for children. As they traveled up the steep slope, 'Abdu'l-Bahá said, "This cable car is like a balloon flying in the air." At the top, they walked along the East-End Lookout, an elegant wooden structure. From there they had a glorious view of the whole city stretching out below.[5]

When May and Sutherland had visited 'Akká in 1909, 'Abdu'l-Bahá had seen May holding one of His grandsons in her arms. He asked her, "You love that baby?"

She replied, "Oh! I love him."

'Abdu'l-Bahá asked, "Would you like to have a baby?"

"I should be so happy to have one—"

They spoke some more on the subject, and May said, "I choose whatever God chooses—I have no choice but His."

"That is the best choice, the Will of God is the best choice." 'Abdu'l-Bahá said, "I will pray for you, that God will send you that which is best for you. Be sure of this, that God will send you that which is best for you—" He repeated that several times.

May and Sutherland's daughter, Mary, was born in 1910. 'Abdu'l-Bahá wrote, "In the garden of existence a rose hath bloomed with the utmost freshness, fragrance and beauty. Educate her according to the divine teachings so that she may grow up to be a real Bahá'í and strive with all thy heart, that she may receive the Holy Spirit."[6]

While 'Abdu'l-Bahá was in Montreal, May told Him, "At the time that I visited 'Akká I despaired of ever having the blessing of children. Praise be to God! My supplications and your prayers at the Holy Shrine of Bahá'u'lláh were accepted and I was blessed with a dear baby."

'Abdu'l-Bahá told her, "Children are the ornaments of the home. A home which has no children is like one without light."[7]

Mary Maxwell was two years old when 'Abdu'l-Bahá visited her home. She would often sit on 'Abdu'l-Bahá's lap, and He would stroke her curls, saying, "She is precious! She is precious!"[8]

One day while He was staying in the Maxwell home, 'Abdu'l-Bahá told His companions, "Today I was resting . . . in my bedroom and the door opened. The little girl came in to me and pushed my eyelids up with her small finger and said, 'Wake up, 'Abdu'l-Bahá!' I took her in my arms and placed her head on my chest and we both had a good sleep."

When May complained to 'Abdu'l-Bahá that Mary was naughty, He said, "Leave her alone. She is the essence of sweetness."[9]

May talked with 'Abdu'l-Bahá about the work of Maria Montessori, an Italian physician who had opened a preschool in Rome in 1907. Dr. Montessori encouraged students to learn by following their own interests. She then trained teachers from around the world in her methods. Later, May hired a Montessori teacher and started Canada's first Montessori school in her home, for Mary and eight other children.

In contrast to the strict traditional schools of the time, May encouraged Mary's inquisitive spirit. She said that her daughter loved everything about nature: "She knows about toads, frogs, lizards, snakes, mud eels, and I don't know what slimy creatures. All this knowledge she has gained at first hand, straight from the source by watching these creatures—catching them—keeping them for a time and feeding them—and then making people read her all about them in books."[10]

As 'Abdu'l-Bahá prepared to leave Montreal, He told the Bahá'ís, "I have sown the seed. You must water it. You must educate the souls in divine morals, make them spiritual and lead them to the oneness of humanity and to universal peace."[11]

Even though 'Abdu'l-Bahá stayed in other homes in America and in Europe, the Maxwell home is the only one considered a Bahá'í shrine. When Mary Maxwell grew up, she married 'Abdu'l-Bahá's grandson, Shoghi Effendi. She later gave the house to the Bahá'ís of Canada. She said, "Things arise in historic perspective as time goes by. This is the only private home in Canada where 'Abdu'l-Bahá stayed. After His visit, it was always considered blessed by having been used by Him. For future generations, it will eventually grow in importance and sacredness, because He, the Centre of the Covenant, the Greatest Mystery of God, stayed here."[12]

28

The Journey West

The Bahá'ís of California had sent telegrams begging 'Abdu'l-Bahá to visit them. Finally, He agreed. In September, He wrote, "It is because the friends of California, and particularly those of San Francisco, have so frequently called and pleaded, expressed despair and wept and sent incessant supplications, that I have determined to go to California."[1]

'Abdu'l-Bahá was exhausted. He said, "How will the great distance to California be traversed? We have no choice, as in the path of God we must regard troubles as blessings and discomforts as greatest bounties."[2] On the journey west, He stopped again in Chicago. He also visited Wisconsin, Minnesota, and Nebraska before reaching Colorado.

In Glenwood Springs, Colorado, 'Abdu'l-Bahá took a rare opportunity for rest. Maḥmúd described the beautiful surroundings outside the Hotel Colorado, which was built in 1893: "Three magnificent mountains stood in the distance on three sides, each crowned with trees and adorned with flowers of many hues. They were like peacock feathers and had a unique beauty from every viewpoint."[3]

'Abdu'l-Bahá visited the Vapor Caves, which are natural underground steam baths that continue to attract many visitors today. Hot mineral water from nearby hot springs flows through the caves. Visitors sit in stone alcoves, breathing the soothing steam vapor. The Ute Indians considered these caves to be a sacred place of healing for centuries. They are the only known natural steam caves in North America. The temperature in the caves is about 110 degrees Fahrenheit, so people visit them for about ten to twelve minutes at a time.

After visiting the caves, 'Abdu'l-Bahá said, "Today I am relieved of fatigue. We have been to many lovely places during this journey but because of our work we had no time to look at the scenery. We did not even think of a moment's rest. Today, however, we have had a little respite."

When He returned to the hotel, He stood in the garden and said, "It would be good to eat here."[4] The hotel manager had the waiters set up a large table in the garden for lunch. 'Abdu'l-Bahá gave the waiters generous tips both before and after lunch.

That afternoon, sad news arrived for 'Abdu'l-Bahá by telegram. Thornton Chase, who lived in Los Angeles, was seriously ill and in the hospital. Thornton was the first Bahá'í in the United States, and he had visited 'Abdu'l-Bahá in 'Akká in 1907. 'Abdu'l-Bahá loved Thornton very much, and was sad to hear of his illness. The group left Glenwood Springs that night.

The train passed through the Rocky Mountains, and Maḥmúd wrote that the mountains rose "like walls from the railway bed, formidable and immense. Gazing at their summits one felt as if the mountains would fall down. There were some special roofless observation cars on the train so that passengers might have a full view of the majestic mountains."[5]

As He passed these lovely scenes, 'Abdu'l-Bahá gave thanks for spiritual aid from Bahá'u'lláh. He said, "Truly, were it not for . . . His assistance, what could I have done? Just one person alone in the east and west of America, in the mountains and wilderness—it is no light matter. . . . See how His aid and favor descend upon us. This trip fills us with wonder! Offer thanks to the Blessed Beauty that He has bestowed such confirmations upon us."[6]

'Abdu'l-Bahá stopped in Salt Lake City, Utah, then arrived in San Francisco on October 1. A group of Bahá'ís welcomed Him at a lovely house He had rented. The house was surrounded by a large garden, and its porch was filled with a variety of fragrant potted flowers and plants. Maḥmúd wrote, "The enthusiasm, eagerness, excitement, joy and singing of the believers surrounded 'Abdu'l-Bahá. . . . These ecstatic friends offered thanks for the bounty of attaining His presence and being near to Him."[7]

'Abdu'l-Bahá sent telegrams to the Bahá'ís in the East, saying, "Rejoicing among friends of God in San Francisco. Truly confirmations are overwhelming and happiness complete."[8]

'Abdu'l-Bahá enjoyed traveling across the San Francisco Bay to Oakland, where gatherings were held at the elegant home of Helen Goodall and her daughter, Ella Goodall Cooper. It was a fifteen-minute ride by ferry. From the boat, the brightly lit buildings of San Francisco could be seen. Maḥmúd wrote, "The splendid buildings and towers adorned with brilliant lights seemed to be golden palaces set with colored jewels. Lights from the homes crowning the high hills appeared like a string of pearls. The Master enjoyed the scene and whenever He went that way He praised it highly."[9]

In 1904, a fifteen-year-old girl named Ramona Allen had been invited to visit Helen Goodall's home with her mother, Frances Orr Allen. Later, Ramona wrote, "That was the most important day of my life."

Helen was a quiet, gentle, and dignified lady with white hair. She spoke in a soft voice and made everyone feel welcome in her home. Her daughter, Ella, had a happy and enthusiastic spirit. They had learned about the Bahá'í Faith in 1898, and Ella had visited 'Abdu'l-Bahá the following year. A Japanese servant named Kanichi Yamamoto, or "Moto," worked in their home, and he was also a Bahá'í.

When Ramona and her mother arrived, Helen and Ella greeted them with radiant and welcoming smiles. They served tea. Then they told their visitors about the Bahá'í Faith and the life of 'Abdu'l-Bahá. It was the first time that Ramona had heard the word "Bahá'í."

Ramona was very interested in religion. Her parents had allowed her to attend various Sunday schools during her spiritual search. Ramona was "spellbound" as she listened to the story of 'Abdu'l-Bahá and the Bahá'í teachings. She later wrote, "I had finally found that for which I had been searching. I turned to my mother and said, 'I believe this!', for I had instantly accepted Bahá'u'lláh and His Teachings. . . . Throughout my life I have never had any doubts."[10]

A few years later, when Ramona was in her late teens, Ella invited her to visit with some of her friends who were interested in the Bahá'í Faith. They began to meet each week. Ella called the group of girls her "Peaches," or "Peach Tree," and they called her "Mother Peach." At the meetings, Moto served them tea, cheese puffs, and cinnamon toast.

The Peaches continued to meet for about fourteen years. Ella told them stories about the Bahá'í Faith, taught them prayers, and shared letters she and her mother received from 'Abdu'l-Bahá. There were very few Bahá'í books available, so many of the teachings and prayers came from copies of letters 'Abdu'l-Bahá wrote to various Bahá'ís.

Ramona and her family eagerly visited 'Abdu'l-Bahá when He arrived in San Francisco. Ramona wrote, "That exhilarating, magic moment of seeing 'Abdu'l-Bahá for the first time was like seeing the sun burst forth through the soft, rosy glow of dawn. . . . He appeared to be enveloped in a beautiful, ethereal, luminous light. The room seemed flooded with sunshine. Flowers were everywhere, and their fragrance filled the air. . . . My heart felt as though it would burst with joy and happiness . . . "

Ramona gave Him some yellow roses from her family's garden. He smiled and thanked her lovingly. She wrote, "His gentle, smiling eyes touched my soul; they seemed to tell me that He knew what was in my heart and everything about me. I felt as though I were in another world."

After He spoke to the group that had gathered, 'Abdu'l-Bahá served them tea in small crystal glasses. Ramona said it was "the most delicious tea I had ever tasted. It was light amber-colored Persian tea which He had brought with Him. To this day I can remember its fragrance and taste its sweetness."

Ramona found that "The happiness of that first meeting has remained with me all of my life. We knew that we were blessed and privileged to be in the presence of 'Abdu'l-Bahá. We were full of deep joy as we basked in His love."[11]

29

Unique One of the Orient

One morning while 'Abdu'l-Bahá was in San Francisco, two Japanese Bahá'ís came to see Him. He said, "This is an historic event. It is out of the ordinary that an Iranian should meet Japanese people in San Francisco with such love and harmony. This is through the power of Bahá'u'lláh and calls for our thankfulness and happiness. . . . The power of Bahá'u'lláh makes all difficulties simple."[1]

That power also brought Kanichi Yamamoto to the Bahá'í Faith, making him the first Japanese Bahá'í in the world. Kanichi, who was called "Moto" by his friends, was born in Japan and raised as a Buddhist, but as a young man, he became a Christian. Then he moved to Honolulu, Hawaii, and worked as a servant. Elizabeth Muther, a young lady who was staying in the home where Moto worked, helped him as he struggled to learn English. When Helen Goodall and her daughter Ella visited Honolulu in 1902, they met with Elizabeth, and Elizabeth soon became a Bahá'í.

Elizabeth told Moto about the Bahá'í Faith. Though he had not yet mastered English, he understood and accepted the Faith immediately. Wanting to be sure, Elizabeth asked Moto how he knew he had found the truth. Moto put his hand on his heart and said he knew it there. Moto said, "Oh, Miss Muther, I am so happy! . . . and I can only say, Oh God! How hast thou honored me to have made me Thy servant!"[2]

Moto was eager to write to 'Abdu'l-Bahá about his acceptance of the Bahá'í Faith. He tried four times to write a letter in English, but he felt unable to express his feelings in his new language. Elizabeth suggested that Moto write to 'Abdu'l-Bahá in Japanese. She told him that 'Abdu'l-Bahá would understand the spirit of his words. When Moto received 'Abdu'l-Bahá's answer, he felt that his letter had been fully answered.

In 1903, Moto went to Oakland to work as a butler for Helen Goodall. The next year, he wrote to 'Abdu'l-Bahá again in Japanese, and Helen sent the letter along with her own.

'Abdu'l-Bahá's secretary said that when this letter from Moto arrived, 'Abdu'l-Bahá jokingly asked him, "Well, do you not know Japanese?"

His secretary said, "No, Master, I hardly know English."

"Then what shall we do with this letter?" 'Abdu'l-Bahá asked with a smile.

"Perhaps you should do with it as you did with the others," was the reply.

'Abdu'l-Bahá said, "Very well. I will turn to Bahá'u'lláh and He will tell me what to say."

In His next letter to Moto, 'Abdu'l-Bahá wrote, "O thou who art the single one of Japan and the unique one of the extreme orient! . . . Arise to guide the people of Japan . . . Do not wonder at the favor and bounty of the Lord. By the favor of God . . . an atom hath become shining like the sun!"[3]

In 1908, Moto's intended bride came to California from Japan. Helen Goodall gave them a beautiful wedding in her ballroom. Many Bahá'ís attended, along with some Japanese friends of the couple. After the ceremony, Moto joked to his wife, "I don't want you to be like a Japanese wife, always bowing. I want you to be like an American wife and boss me!"[4]

When 'Abdu'l-Bahá came to California, Moto served Him in His rented house. Moto also arranged for 'Abdu'l-Bahá to speak to the members of the Japanese Young Men's Christian Association (YMCA) of Oakland. The meeting was held at the Japanese Independent Church. It began with a Bible reading and hymn in Japanese, followed by a prayer. Then Mr. Kanno, a Japanese poet and philosopher, spoke in 'Abdu'l-Bahá's honor.

When 'Abdu'l-Bahá spoke, His Persian words were first translated into English by His companion, Dr. Faríd. Then the English was translated into Japanese by the pastor of the church, Reverend Kazahira. Frances Orr Allen called it "a marvelous mingling of the East and the West and the Islands of the Sea."[5] 'Abdu'l-Bahá encouraged them to promote peace and unity:

It is a great happiness to be here this evening, especially for the reason that the members of this Association have come from the region of the Orient. For a long time I have entertained a desire to meet some of the Japanese friends. That nation has achieved extraordinary progress in a short space of time . . . they must assuredly possess the capacity for spiritual development. . . .

All war and conflict, bloodshed and battle, every form of sedition has been due to some form of prejudice—whether religious, racial or national. . . . Prejudice is a destroyer of the foundations of the world of humanity, whereas religion was meant to be the cause of fellowship and agreement. . . .

Religion purifies the hearts. Religion impels men to achieve praiseworthy deeds. Religion becomes the cause of love in human hearts, for religion is a divine foundation, the foundation ever conducive to life. . . . Religion is ever constructive, not destructive. . . .

Blessed souls—whether Moses, Jesus, Zoroaster, Krishna, Buddha, Confucius or Muḥammad—were the cause of the illumination of the world of humanity. How can we deny such irrefutable proof? How can we be blind to such light? . . . We ourselves must investigate reality and be fair in judgment. . . .

And ye who are the people of the Orient. . . . Ye must become brilliant lamps. Ye must shine as stars radiating the light of love toward all mankind. May you be the cause of love amongst the nations. Thus may the world become witness that the Orient has ever been the dawning point of illumination, the source of love and reconciliation.[6]

After He spoke, 'Abdu'l-Bahá walked down the aisle of the room, and mothers held out their babies to be blessed. They smiled happily when He said in English, "Good baby; Japanese baby."[7]

At another meeting with some Japanese visitors, 'Abdu'l-Bahá said, "I hope that you will become heavenly and not just be a Japanese, an Arab, an Englishman or a Persian, Turk or American; that you will become divine and bring your life into accord with the teachings of Bahá'u'lláh. Observe: I am one of the servants of Bahá'u'lláh, helpless and weak but as I am under the shadow of His teachings you see what confirmations descend upon me."[8]

* * *

"Religion was meant to be the cause of fellowship and agreement. . . ."
— *'Abdu'l-Bahá*

30

At the Home of Science

Lua Getsinger was among the Bahá'ís who were overjoyed to welcome 'Abdu'l-Bahá to California. She wrote to a friend, "How much more than a <u>thousand</u> times I am repaid for all the work I have done here the last year and a half!" She felt that she had planted seeds of faith, and that "He has watered my garden . . . with such a power as to produce in a single day and night the most wonderful flowers and fruit."

When 'Abdu'l-Bahá visited Leland Stanford Junior University in Palo Alto, California, on October 8, Lua called it "a most wonderful day."[1] About 1800 students and 180 professors, along with other leaders, gathered to hear Him.

Stanford University was founded by Leland and Jane Stanford. Leland had made a fortune in the railroad business, had been elected the governor of California, and had served on the United States Senate for eight years. The couple's only child, Leland Stanford Jr., died of typhoid fever at age fifteen, and the school was established in his memory.

Stanford University opened its doors in 1891. Stanford was unusual because it allowed both women and men to attend, at a time when most colleges were for men only. It was also not associated with a religious organization, like most other universities.

Stanford's first president, David Starr Jordan, still held that position at the time of 'Abdu'l-Bahá's visit. Jordan was a brilliant scientist and administrator. He also traveled and spoke about world peace, in addition to publishing a number of books.

While introducing 'Abdu'l-Bahá, Dr. Jordan, said, "It is our portion to have with us, through the courtesy of our Persian friends, one of the great religious teachers of the world. . . .

"He has upwards of three millions of people following along the lines in which he leads. It is not exactly a new religion, however. The religion of brotherhood, of good will, of friendship between men and nations—*that* is as old as good thinking and good living may be. It may be said in some sense to be the oldest of religions."[2]

'Abdu'l-Bahá then spoke to the audience gathered that day:

The greatest attainment in the world of humanity has ever been scientific in nature. It is the discovery of the realities of things. Inasmuch as I find myself in the home of science—for this is one of the great universities of the country and well known abroad—I feel a keen sense of joy.

The highest praise is due to men who devote their energies to science, and the noblest center is a center wherein the sciences and arts are taught and studied. . . .

According to the limitations of his physical powers man was intended by creation to live upon the earth, but through the exercise of his mental faculties, he removes the restriction of this law and soars in the air like a bird. He penetrates the secrets of the sea in submarines and builds fleets to sail at will over the ocean's surface, commanding the laws of nature to do his will. All the sciences and arts we now enjoy and utilize were once mysteries. . . .

For example, electricity was once a hidden, or latent, natural force. It would have remained hidden if the human intellect had not discovered it. . . . The East can communicate with the West in a few minutes. . . . Man takes the human voice and stores it in a phonograph. . . . Man has broken the laws of nature and is constantly taking out of nature's laboratory new and wonderful things. . . .

I supplicate God that He may confirm and assist you, that each one of you may become a professor . . . in the world of scientific knowledge, a faithful standard-bearer of peace. . . .

It is my hope that you who are students in this university may . . . enjoy the most perfect companionship one with another, even as one family—as brothers, sisters, fathers, mothers—associating together in peace and true fellowship.[3]

After His talk, Maḥmúd said, "the entire audience was overcome with admiration. The applause shook the building to its very foundation." Dr. Jordan said, "We are all under very great obligation to 'Abdu'l-Bahá for this illuminating expression of the brotherhood of man and the value of international peace. I think we can best show our appreciation by simply a rising vote of thanks." The audience stood and clapped their hands and stomped their feet to show their appreciation for 'Abdu'l-Bahá's talk.[4]

On Friday, November 1, the local newspaper, *The Palo Altan*, was entirely devoted to 'Abdu'l-Bahá's visit. One article reported, "It seemed to be a notable day when Abdul-Baha from the far country of the Orient met Dr. David Starr Jordan of the far western shore, both carrying the standard of international peace and universal brotherhood. . . . Abdul-Baha carries the message of religion and Doctor Jordan carries the message of science, both aiming for one great result. As all men are the children of one God, so are they all brothers, and we are at the dawning of a new day when the relationship of world fraternity will be seen and recognized."[5]

'Abdu'l-Bahá wrote to the editor of *The Palo Altan*, Mr. H.W. Simkins, saying, "At the time I met you and felt the susceptibilities of your conscience my heart and soul became greatly attached. . . . Your visit gave me the utmost happiness. The address delivered in Stanford University and published completely in your paper was observed today—and on account of it I became both pleased and grateful. . . . I shall never forget your cordiality, and as long as life lasts I shall remember you. I beg of God, that that dear friend (yourself) may become like unto a shining star in the horizon of Reality, and become the cause of bestowing spiritual life upon the world of humanity."[6]

Lua Getsinger felt revitalized by 'Abdu'l-Bahá's visit. She said that "His pure and holy thought—became crystallized jewels of speech—

scattered so profusely as to transform Cal[ifornia]—from the Golden State to the Diamond State—leaving every searching heart therein studded with precious gems."[7]

31

Unity among Religions

Maḥmud called ʻAbduʼl-Baháʼs talk on October 12 "unique and magnificent. . . . Indeed, it can be counted as a miracle."[1] That was the day that ʻAbduʼl-Bahá spoke to two thousand people at the Jewish Temple Emanu-El in San Francisco.

The Congregation Emanu-El, as it is known today, was established in 1850, one of the first two Jewish temples in the city. In 1926, the congregation moved to a majestic new building that remains a landmark today.

Maḥmúd was impressed that many of the Jewish people, who did not accept that Jesus or Muḥammad were Messengers of God, gave a warm reception to ʻAbduʼl-Bahá, who came to introduce them to yet another divine Prophet. The leader of the congregation, Rabbi Martin Meyer, introduced ʻAbduʼl-Bahá with great respect, saying, "It is our privilege and a very high privilege indeed to welcome in our midst this morning Abdul-Baha, a great teacher of our age and generation.

"The heart of the Orient seems to be essentially religious . . . and now and again, out of the heart of the Orient the fundamental religious message of the world is stated and restated. Abdul-Baha is the representative of one of the religious systems of life. . . . I know that what he will say will be of significance to us."[2]

Ramona Allen was among the audience that day. She reported that 'Abdu'l-Bahá stood "between two lovely palm trees while a shaft of light from a window fell across Him and bathed Him in the morning sunshine."[3] He urged everyone present to join together in unity:

The greatest bestowal of God in the world of humanity is religion. . . . Religion confers upon man eternal life. . . . It opens the doors of unending happiness and bestows everlasting honor upon the human kingdom. . . .

I wish you to be fair and reasonable in your judgment, setting aside all religious prejudices. . . .

Today the Christians are believers in Moses, accept Him as a Prophet of God and praise Him most highly. The Muslims are, likewise, believers in Moses, accept the validity of His Prophethood, at the same time believing in Christ. . . . What harm could result to the Jewish people, then, if they in return should accept Christ and acknowledge the validity of the Prophethood of Muḥammad? . . .

. . . You would lose nothing by such action and statement. On the contrary, you would contribute to the welfare of mankind. You would be instrumental in establishing the happiness of the world of humanity. . . . Our God is one God and the Creator of all mankind. . . . We acknowledge Him as a God of kindness, justice and mercy. Why then should we, His children and followers, war and fight, bringing sorrow and grief into the hearts of each other? God is loving and merciful. His intention in religion has ever been the bond of unity and affinity between humankind. . . .

The age has dawned when human fellowship will become a reality.

The century has come when all religions shall be unified.

The dispensation is at hand when all nations shall enjoy the blessings of international peace. . . .

For all mankind shall dwell in peace and security beneath the shelter of the great tabernacle of the one living God.[4]

After His talk, many people greeted 'Abdu'l-Bahá and thanked Him. Later, when 'Abdu'l-Bahá met with the Bahá'ís at Helen Goodall and Ella Goodall Cooper's home, He commented, "From the beginning of Christianity and Islam up to the present day, no one has spoken thus, proving the validity of Christ and Muḥammad in a Jewish temple and in a manner to which no one took exception. Rather, most were appreciative and content. This is none other than the assistance of Bahá'u'lláh."[5]

Maḥmud said, "The effect and influence of the address were such that from then on there was evidence of unity and communication between the Christians and Jews. They even made plans to visit each other's places of worship to give talks about the unity of peoples and religions. Whenever they met 'Abdu'l-Bahá or attended Bahá'í gatherings, they expressed their gratitude from the depths of their hearts for this great Cause and its new teachings."[6]

That afternoon, a special event for children had been planned. The rooms were filled with children and their parents and friends. The children sang a hymn, and 'Abdu'l-Bahá gave them candy and flowers. Then He gave each child and adult an envelope of rose leaves. Frances Orr Allen, Ramona Allen's mother, wrote, "It was a beautiful afternoon. Truly one who has not seen Abdul-Baha with the children has missed a great deal."[7]

The following day, 'Abdu'l-Bahá spoke at a reading room for the blind. Children and youth from a school in Berkeley and adults from an Oakland home joined the gathering. 'Abdu'l-Bahá told them that by being educated, the blind are given sight. He said that they must not be sad, because they had *insight,* which is divine and can see the beauty of God.

On the evening of October 16, over one hundred Bahá'ís gathered for a wonderful feast at the Goodall home. "The beautiful rooms were filled with tables, adorned with yellow chrysanthemums and pyramids of fruit. . . . Abdu'l-Baha requested that we partake of the food so bountifully provided, while he walked about speaking words of wisdom and love, giving us the spiritual food, for which we hungered. . . . It was the most spiritual meeting. Gathered under one roof were people of different nations and various nationalities, the young and old, all meeting in love and fellowship, and in devotion to the Servant of God in this day."[8]

'Abdu'l-Bahá spent several days giving public talks and meeting with individuals and small groups. He said He was very pleased with San Francisco and enjoyed visiting Golden Gate Park. He especially liked looking at the growing flowers and walking along the shore of small lakes.

The Bahá'ís of Portland, Oregon, and Seattle, Washington, had begged 'Abdu'l-Bahá to visit them, but He said it was impossible, because the distance was so great. He reassured them, "Send my love and good wishes to all the friends in Portland and Seattle and tell them that I am always with them. Meeting physically is as nothing compared with spiritual bonds. What is important is spiritual nearness."[9]

Nevertheless, when they received this message, the Bahá'ís in those cities came to San Francisco to meet 'Abdu'l-Bahá. They were unable to resist the opportunity to meet Him and experience His all-encompassing love. 'Abdu'l-Bahá expressed His feelings in this way: "In my heart there is such love for the heavenly friends that I do not wish even a speck of dust to touch them. God forbid! If I see harm coming to one of you, I will throw myself in its path to shield you."[10]

* * *

"The age has dawned when human fellowship will become a reality."
— *'Abdu'l-Bahá*

32

A Firm Believer

In July, while in New Hampshire, 'Abdu'l-Bahá had written to Thornton Chase, who lived in California. 'Abdu'l-Bahá called him "my ancient Friend: my Companion and Associate." He told Thornton, "Every day thou art remembered by me, and thy services are reviewed before mine eyes, and my good pleasure in thee is increased. In reality, thou hast labored hard in the Kingdom of God and thou hast undertaken infinite trouble. Thou didst become the cause of the guidance of many people."[1]

'Abdu'l-Bahá said that Thornton Chase was the first Bahá'í in America. Thornton became a Bahá'í in 1894, when he was in his late forties and living in Chicago. He longed to join the first Americans who visited 'Abdu'l-Bahá, but he was unable to get time off from his work with an insurance company. Still, Thornton wrote to 'Abdu'l-Bahá, and 'Abdu'l-Bahá responded, "While thou art in that far distant country . . . I see thee with the eye of the heart as though thou were present here. . . ."[2]

Thornton had always been deeply interested in religion. He had also experienced many difficulties in his life. While still a teenager, he had served in the Union Army during the Civil War. Afterward, he went to college for a time, and then worked in his father's lumber company. Thornton started his own lumber business, but it soon failed. He then spent about sixteen years seeking steady work in different parts of the country. He was employed as an actor, a schoolteacher, a singing tutor, and a newspaper editor, among other jobs. Thornton had a marvelous singing voice and was involved in church choirs and music clubs. He was also a published poet. He even invented a mining tool and found silver in the San Juan Mountains of Colorado. Finally, he achieved success in the insurance business.

Thornton traveled a great deal in his work, and he spent much of his time on those trips meeting with Bahá'ís and giving talks about the Bahá'í Faith. He and 'Abdu'l-Bahá continued to write to each other. Thornton helped organize the Bahá'í community of Chicago. He also helped start the Bahá'í Publishing Society to publish Bahá'í materials in English. To advance this work, he edited manuscripts, helped translators, and wrote pamphlets and books.

In 1907, Thornton was able to join some friends on a journey to 'Akká. He was overjoyed to be meeting 'Abdu'l-Bahá after having to postpone the trip for so long because of his work. 'Abdu'l-Bahá greeted him and embraced Thornton warmly, like a father welcoming His son. Thornton said, "Our hearts were full of joyful tears, because we were 'at home.' His welcoming spirit banished strangeness, as though we had always known him. It was as if, after long journeyings, weariness, trials and searchings, we had at last reached home."

Thornton said, "I found in Abdul-Baha a man, strong, powerful, without a thought as to any act, as free and unstilted as a father with his family or a boy with playmates. Yet each movement, his walk, his greeting, his sitting down and rising up were eloquent of power, full of dignity. . . . He extends love to every one; he draws near to them; he invites them; he loves to serve them, even in little things. . . . He is gentle but not weak; sweet and powerful; humble and mighty; . . ."[3]

Thornton also noted, "In Abdul-Baha is never a trace of self-interest. Each thought, each word of his is for the universal love, the divinity of man in his oneness with mankind. He speaks not from the self, but from the Spirit; yet his speech is that of the man, simple, direct, as of a father to his son. 'Are you well?' 'Are you happy?' This would be an oft repeated greeting."[4]

Thornton and his friends viewed a photograph of Bahá'u'lláh, which Thornton called a "great privilege." Out of reverence for Bahá'u'lláh as a Messenger of God, His photograph is not displayed publicly. His photograph is kept at the Bahá'í International Archives in Haifa, Israel, and is shown to Bahá'ís when they visit the Bahá'í World Center on pilgrimage. Thornton wrote, "It is a majestic face, that of a strong, powerful, stern man, yet filled with an indescribable sweetness."[5]

Later, 'Abdu'l-Bahá told Thornton's group, "You have seen the picture of the Blessed Perfection, and also Abdul-Baha, and we love you. You must be very glad and we are very glad. I hope the influence of this great thing will appear, and that, when you return to America, by you the Americans will be made happy."[6]

When he returned to the United States, Thornton wrote a book to share his experiences with the Bahá'ís. A short time later, Thornton received a remarkable gift from 'Abdu'l-Bahá—a new name. 'Abdu'l-Bahá called him <u>Th</u>ábit, or "the Firm." He explained, "Today the greatest of all affairs in the Cause is firmness and steadfastness. A tree will not give fruit unless it be firmly rooted. A foundation will not last unless it be firm. . . . For this reason I have named thee Thahbet [<u>Th</u>ábit] (meaning firmness) and I ask the True One and supplicate Him that thou shalt remain firm in the Cause of God as an unshakable mountain and that the whirlwinds of test shall never have any effect upon thee; nay, rather that thou shalt be the cause of the firmness of others."[7]

About two years later, Thornton's company moved him to a new position in California, at about half his salary. For years, his employers had been unhappy about the amount of time he focused on the Bahá'í Faith. But as his work took him on frequent travels throughout the West, Thornton often met with and encouraged the Bahá'ís in many communities.

'Abdu'l-Bahá wrote to him, "Be thou not sad nor unhappy on account of the incidents which have transpired. As these trials have come to you in the Path of God, therefore they must become the cause of your happiness and rejoicing. . . . All these things shall pass away. What remains and lasts is the eternal glory and everlasting life, and those trials shall be the cause of universal progress and development."[8]

In 1911, when 'Abdu'l-Bahá visited Europe, some American Bahá'ís went there to meet Him. Thornton wrote, "It was a sorrow to me that I could not go, but it matters not so much, the physical meeting. He who strives to be of service in God's work actually meets Abdul-Baha (the Servant of God), because he enters upon the plane of divine service."[9]

Thornton had hoped to visit Chicago while 'Abdu'l-Bahá was there, but business had kept him in California. Finally, along with the other Bahá'ís of California, Thornton eagerly awaited 'Abdu'l-Bahá's arrival in San Francisco. But another physical meeting was not to be. Thornton became ill while on a business trip and had to be hospitalized. On September 30, the day before 'Abdu'l-Bahá reached San Francisco, Thornton Chase passed away.

On October 18, 'Abdu'l-Bahá took a train from San Francisco to Los Angeles. When He arrived in Los Angeles, several church and society leaders invited Him to speak, but He said kindly, "I have absolutely no time. I have come here to visit Mr. Chase's grave and to meet the friends. I will stay here one or two days and then I must leave."[10]

The next day, 'Abdu'l-Bahá and about twenty-five Bahá'ís went to Inglewood Park Cemetery near Los Angeles to visit Thornton's grave. 'Abdu'l-Bahá walked straight to the gravesite without asking for its location. He spread the flowers on the grave with intense love and affection. He raised His hands toward heaven and prayed. Then He praised Thornton's character:

Mr. Chase was of the blessed souls. The best time of his life was spent in the path of God. He had no other aim except the good pleasure of the Lord and no other desire except the attainment to the Kingdom of God. During his lifetime he bore many trials and vicissitudes, but he was very patient and long-suffering. He had a heart most illuminated, a spirit most rejoiced; his hope was to serve the world of humanity; . . . This is a personage who will not be forgotten. For the present his worth is not known but in the future it will be inestimably dear. His sun will ever be shining, his stars will ever bestow the light. The people will honor this grave. Therefore, the friends of God must visit this grave and on my behalf bring flowers and seek the sublimity of the spiritual station for him and have the utmost consideration for the members of his family. This personage will not be forgotten."[11]

Before He left, 'Abdu'l-Bahá placed His forehead on the grave and kissed it, bringing tears to everyone's eyes.

'Abdu'l-Bahá returned to San Francisco for a few days. When it was time for Him to depart, His house was filled with Bahá'ís. When they heard Him coming downstairs, they all stood and cried out "Alláh-u-Abhá!" 'Abdu'l-Bahá was touched by the devotion of the Bahá'ís. He anointed each person with attar of rose. Then He said:

Here I want to bid you farewell. This meeting and assemblage are very moving. This is the last draught in the goblet! How thankful we must be to the Blessed Perfection that He has brought the hearts so near to each other. This attar that I give you is but a token of the fragrance of the Abhá Paradise—the best of all fragrances. I am very sad to be separated from you and I do not know how to express it. It is not possible to give tongue to the feelings of the heart. I am greatly moved because I saw the love of Bahá'u'lláh in you, I witnessed the light of Bahá'u'lláh in your beings. I am so moved that I cannot speak. I leave it to your hearts to feel what I feel. Although I am going away from you, you have your place in my heart. I will never forget you. When I reach the Shrine of Bahá'u'lláh, I shall lay my head on the Sacred Threshold and beseech confirmation for every one of the friends.[12]

* * *

"Although I am going away from you, you have your place in my heart. I will never forget you."

—'Abdu'l-Bahá

33

Gatherings of Unity

When 'Abdu'l-Bahá was getting ready to return to Haifa after his long journey, a farewell banquet was planned at the Great Northern Hotel in New York on November 23. About three hundred people attended, wearing formal attire. The hall was decorated with banners, and the Greatest Name, a version of the name "Bahá" in Arabic calligraphy, was hung above the stage. Long rectangular tables were set up for dining, and small tables at the sides of the room were filled with colorful flowers, desserts, and crystal glassware.

When 'Abdu'l-Bahá entered, everyone rose and called out, "Alláh-u-Abhá!" 'Abdu'l-Bahá spoke about the oneness of humanity:

This meeting of yours tonight . . . is a universal gathering; it is heavenly and divine in purpose because it serves the oneness of the world of humanity and promotes international peace. . . . It promotes love and fraternity among all humankind, seeks to abolish and destroy barriers which separate the human family, proclaims the equality of man and woman . . . removes racial, national and religious prejudices and establishes the foundation of the heavenly Kingdom in the hearts of all nations and peoples. . . .

Consecrate and devote yourselves to the betterment and service of all the human race. Let no barrier of ill feeling or personal prejudice exist between these souls, for when your motives are universal and your intentions heavenly in character . . . you will become the recipients of the bounty and good pleasure of God.

This meeting is, verily, the noblest and most worthy of all meetings in the world because of these underlying spiritual and universal purposes. Such a banquet and assemblage command the sincere devotion of all present and invite the downpouring of the blessings of God. Therefore, be ye assured and confident that the confirmations of God are descending upon you, the assistance of God will be given unto you . . . the fragrant breezes of the rose gardens of divine mercy will waft through the windows of your souls. Be ye confident and steadfast; your services are confirmed by the powers of heaven, for your intentions are lofty, your purposes pure and worthy. God is the helper of those souls whose aim is to serve humanity and whose efforts and endeavors are devoted to the good and betterment of all mankind.[1]

Juliet Thompson wrote, "Just before the food was served the Master rose from His seat, a vial of attar of rose in His hand, and passed among all the tables, anointing every one of His guests. As His wonderful hand, dripping perfume, touched my forehead, as He scattered on my hair the fragrant drops, my whole being seemed to wake and sparkle."[2]

Maḥmúd wrote, "Many of the hotel guests saw the banquet and were astonished to see the grandeur of the Master and the sincerity and enthusiasm of the friends." The hotel staff was also curious. "They came to see the Master to ask about the banquet and why so many distinguished Americans were praising and glorifying a person from the East. Indeed, it was a banquet for a king and a source of awakening to every person of insight."[3]

Unjustly, the owner of the Great Northern Hotel had refused to let the African American Baháʼís attend the banquet. The more the Baháʼís tried to change his mind, the more decisive he became. He claimed that if people saw African Americans entering the hotel, "no respectable person will ever set foot in it and my business will go to the winds."[4]

Because of this racist attitude, a special feast was arranged for the African American Baháʼís at the home of Carrie and Edward Kinney. Many white women served their black friends with love and kindness. ʻAbduʼl-Bahá said:

Today you have carried out the laws of the Blessed Beauty and have truly acted according to the teachings of the Supreme Pen. Behold what an influence and effect the words of Baháʼuʼlláh have had upon the hearts, that hating and shunning have been forgotten and that prejudices have been obliterated to such an extent that you arose to serve one another with great sincerity.[5]

A few days earlier, some children had seen 'Abdu'l-Bahá on their way home from school, and asked about Him. Juliet Thompson had invited them to the Kinney home to meet Him. When they arrived, 'Abdu'l-Bahá spoke to them with great kindness. He gave them candies and flowers, and sprinkled them with attar of rose. Then He encouraged them, saying:

> I hope that you will be educated as you ought to be and that each of you will become the pride of your family. May God assist you to acquire divine knowledge in the school of the world of humanity. I shall pray for you and beg assistance for you. Truly, the hearts of the children are very pure. This was why Christ said, "Be ye like children." Praise be to God who created you illumined children. Praise be to the Lord who hath created His creatures perfectly. God has created you as human beings so that you may daily acquire better morals and human virtues. You must obey your parents so that they may be pleased with you, and so that God will be pleased with you, and that you may become the children of the Kingdom and mirror forth the words of Christ.[6]

* * *

"Consecrate and devote yourselves to the betterment and service of all the human race."

—*'Abdu'l-Bahá*

34

Become Brilliant Lamps

Before 'Abdu'l-Bahá left New York, the Bahá'ís wanted to give Him some money for His trip back home, but He would not accept it. He said, "Distribute it among the poor on my behalf. It will be as though I have given it to them. But the most acceptable gift to me is the unity of the believers, service to the Cause of God, diffusion of the divine fragrances and adherence to the counsels of the Abhá Beauty."[1]

The Bahá'ís gathered gifts for 'Abdu'l-Bahá's sister, Bahíyyih Khánum, and other women of His household. He told them:

I am most grateful for your services; in truth you have served me. You have extended hospitality. Night and day you have been ready to serve and to diffuse the divine fragrances. I shall never forget your services, for you have no purpose but the will of God and you desire no station but entry into the Kingdom of God. Now you have brought presents for the members of my family.

They are most acceptable and excellent but better than all these are the gifts of the love of God which remain preserved in the treasuries of the heart. . . . . These jewels must be kept in boxes and vaults and they will eventually perish but those jewels remain in the treasuries of the heart and will remain throughout the world of God for eternity. Thus I will take to them your love, which is the greatest of all gifts. . . .

I, however, have accepted your gifts; but I entrust them to you for you [to] sell and send the proceeds to the fund for the Mashriqu'l-Adhkár in Chicago.[2]

On the morning of December 5, many Bahá'ís from New York and other cities came to the S.S. *Celtic* to say good-bye. There were so many visitors that they filled the first class lounge, and more were standing and sitting outside the lounge. Mahmúd wrote, "The sobs and lamentations of both the young and the old could be heard from afar. . . . As He moved among the friends, the Master spoke to them words of exhortation and admonition, consoling their hearts as He bade them farewell."[3]

'Abdu'l-Bahá's visitors on the ship included Juliet Thompson, Carrie and Edward Kinney, 'Alí Kulí Khán and his wife, Florence, and Agnes Parsons. He left them with these words:

This is my last meeting with you, for now I am on the ship ready to sail away. These are my final words of exhortation. . . .

The earth is one native land, one home; and all mankind are the children of one Father. God has created them, and they are the recipients of His compassion. Therefore, if anyone offends another, he offends God. It is the wish of our heavenly Father that every heart should rejoice and be filled with happiness, that we should live together in felicity and joy. The obstacle to human happiness is racial or religious prejudice, the competitive struggle for existence and inhumanity toward each other. . . .

Beware lest ye offend any heart, lest ye speak against anyone in his absence, lest ye estrange yourselves from the servants of God. You must consider all His servants as your own family and relations. Direct your whole effort toward the happiness of those who are despondent, bestow food upon the hungry, clothe the needy, and glorify the humble. Be a helper to every helpless one, and manifest kindness to your fellow creatures in order that ye may attain the good pleasure of God. . . .

It is my hope that you may become successful in this high calling so that like brilliant lamps you may cast light upon the world of humanity and quicken and stir the body of existence like unto a spirit of life. This is eternal glory. This is everlasting felicity. This is immortal life. This is heavenly attainment. This is being created in the image and likeness of God. And unto this I call you, praying to God to strengthen and bless you.[4]

* * *

"It is the wish of our heavenly Father that every heart should rejoice and be filled with happiness, that we should live together in felicity and joy."
— *'Abdu'l-Bahá*

Discussion Questions

Share these questions with friends and family to spark meaningful conversations about the words and actions of 'Abdu'l-Bahá. You may also want to use them as a springboard for individual reflection, writing, or art.

Chapter 1: Arrival
'Abdu'l-Bahá said, "freedom is not a matter of place, it is a condition. When one is released from the prison of self, that is indeed a release" (p. 9). What does it mean to be imprisoned by self? What might help to release us from the prison of self?

'Abdu'l-Bahá said that to be a Bahá'í means to "love all the world" (p. 9). What are some ways you can put love into action in your community?

How can we extend love beyond our own family and friends to encompass "all the world"?

Chapter 2: City of Love

'Abdu'l-Bahá said He hoped New York would "advance spiritually and become a city of love" (p. 15). What would a city of love look like?

What would your city or town be like if it advanced spiritually? What's a small step you can take to help move toward that goal?

'Abdu'l-Bahá told Howard Colby Ives that it takes "a great deal of courage" to speak of truth (p. 18). What's a situation where you might need courage to speak the truth?

Chapter 3: The First Call to Peace

'Abdu'l-Bahá said, "Material civilization is like unto the lamp, while spiritual civilization is the light in that lamp" (p. 23). What does that mean to you?

What are some examples of material civilization? What are examples of spiritual civilization?

Chapter 4: The Blessed Poor

'Abdu'l-Bahá enjoyed giving money to the poor. Describe a time when you felt good after being generous to someone else.

'Abdu'l-Bahá said the poor are blessed and the "treasures of God" are in their reach (p. 28). What do you think these "treasures of God" might be?

What's one small way you can help the poor in your community?

Chapter 5: Boys of the Bowery

The face of 'Abdu'l-Bahá lit up when an African American boy came to visit Him (p. 32). He noticed and admired racial differences. Is it common in your family or community to talk about racial differences?

When you're among people of other races or backgrounds, do you talk about racial diversity? Why or why not?

What could you do to increase your understanding of racial justice issues in your community?

Chapter 6: A Luminous Star

Soon after learning that alcohol is prohibited in the Bahá'í Faith, John Bosch retired from the wine business. What are some ways that alcohol can have a negative impact on individuals, families, or communities?

What are some positive results that can result from avoiding alcohol and other drugs?

'Abdu'l-Bahá often gave someone a new name, as He did for John Bosch. What is the significance of having a new name?

If you took a new name, what virtue or positive quality would you like it to express? (For example, John Bosch's name, Núrání, means "Luminous.")

Chapter 7: Flowers in a Garden

'Abdu'l-Bahá spoke about the beauty of racial diversity. What are some ways that diversity enriches your life or your community?

Racial conflict is "unworthy" of humanity, according to 'Abdu'l-Bahá (p. 46). What are some actions that might be worthy of or consistent with the noble human spirit?

Chapter 8: Union of East and West

'Alí Kulí <u>Kh</u>án was initially suspicious of the Bahá'í Faith, but he changed his mind and became devoted to it. What's a big change that you've made at some point in your life, and how did it impact you?

At a luncheon in Washington, D.C., 'Abdu'l-Bahá welcomed Louis Gregory and gave him a position of honor at the table. Have you ever stood up for someone who was being treated unfairly? How did that feel?

What are some ways you like to make your guests feel welcome?

Chapter 9: The Titanic Disaster

'Abdu'l-Bahá said "the worlds of God are infinite" and that death is like a birth into a new world (p. 62). How might thinking about death in this way influence our feelings about it?

According to 'Abdu'l-Bahá, death is a release to "a world of unending bliss and joy" (p. 62). How is that different from the way people often speak about death in conversation or in the media?

Chapter 10: Pure Hearts

The art of music is "the food of the soul and spirit," and through it our spirits are uplifted, 'Abdu'l-Bahá said (p. 67). What are some songs or types of music that affect you significantly?

Do you sing or play a musical instrument? If so, how do you feel when practicing this art?

'Abdu'l-Bahá said children have "pure hearts" (p. 67). What does that mean to you? How might someone with a pure heart behave?

Chapter 11: Suffering and Glory

'Abdu'l-Bahá said that "prejudices are vanishing" (p. 72). What are some prejudices that have diminished in our world? What prejudices are still with us?

What are some things you can do to be aware of and remove your own prejudices?

Chapter 12: Temple of Unity

'Abdu'l-Bahá prayed for America to "become glorious in spiritual degrees" (p. 83). What would that look like, in the U.S. or in another country?

'Abdu'l-Bahá asked God to confirm America to upraise the oneness humanity and promulgate the Most Great Peace (p. 83). What could you do to make progress toward those goals, either in the U.S. or in another country?

Chapter 13: The Cornerstone

Nettie Tobin endured a long struggle to move the cornerstone to the site of the Bahá'í House of Worship, and she asked for help from others. Have you ever had to struggle to achieve an important goal? What did you learn from that experience?

'Abdu'l-Bahá said, "The Temple is already built" (p. 90). What does that mean to you?

The cornerstone at the Bahá'í House of Worship for North America is a simple, irregularly shaped stone. Why do you think such a stone was chosen for this important honor?

Chapter 14: Shining Stars

'Abdu'l-Bahá said, "the imperfect eye beholds imperfections" and "the eye that covers faults looks toward the Creator of souls" (p. 93). What does that mean to you?

What are some ways we can avoid focusing on the imperfections of others? What is a helpful way to look at our own imperfections?

Chapter 15: A Treasured Gift

Dr. Zia Baghdadi went to great lengths to bring 'Abdu'l-Bahá a gift for His host. What's a gift you gave or received that made you especially happy?

'Abdu'l-Bahá told a story about a group of rats and mice that didn't have the courage to hang a bell on the cat. He said that no one wants to "hang a bell" on world leaders to establish peace (p. 100). What does that mean to you?

What's a small step you can take to build peace in your family or community?

Chapter 16: Wings of a Bird

'Abdu'l-Bahá said "force is losing its weight" while "mental alertness, intuition, and the spiritual qualities of love and service, in which woman is strong" are gaining influence (pp. 105–6). What are some examples of how these qualities are valued today?

Women and men are compared to two wings of a bird that need to be equal in strength for the bird to fly (p. 108). What are some ways you can help to advance the equality of women and men?

Chapter 17: A Blessed Anniversary

'Abdu'l-Bahá shared His birthday cake with boys he met in the park (p. 110). How is this different from the ways people often celebrate birthdays? How is it similar?

The Day of the Covenant was established because the Bahá'ís wanted a way to celebrate 'Abdu'l-Bahá. What are some things we can do to honor 'Abdu'l-Bahá on that holy day?

Chapter 18: The Portrait

The Bahá'í Faith teaches that art is the same as worship. How might that impact our thoughts and feelings when creating art?

What are some ways you like to create art or use your creativity? Do you think of it as worship? Why or why not?

Chapter 19: Roses of God's Garden

'Abdu'l-Bahá revealed a prayer asking for children to be educated. Why is education so important?

One teaching of Bahá'u'lláh is this: "Regard man as a mine rich in gems of inestimable value. Education can, alone, cause it to reveal its treasures, and enable mankind to benefit therefrom." What does that mean to you?

What are some examples of "gems" you've discovered within yourself?

Chapter 20: Creating a Precious Relic

When a film of 'Abdu'l-Bahá was created, it was said "The beloved friends one hundred years from now will be able to see the form, face, and actions" of 'Abdu'l-Bahá "and even more, listen to the actual tone of his voice . . ." (p. 126). Have you seen this film? If so, how did it impact you?

What gift would you like to give to people living one hundred years from now?

Chapter 21: City of the Covenant

Because of the Covenant, which is the agreement between Bahá'u'lláh and His followers, the Bahá'í Faith has not broken into different groups. How does that fact influence the Bahá'í community?

'Abdu'l-Bahá asked Lua Getsinger to visit and care for a poor friend who was sick. What are some ways that you can help people in your community who are in need?

Chapter 22: Unity Feast

'Abdu'l-Bahá shared coins and kind greetings with about one hundred people every week. He also visited the sick. What are some ways you can show kindness to others in your family or community?

'Abdu'l-Bahá said, "like candles these souls will become ignited and made radiant through the lights of supreme guidance" (p. 138). What do you think it means to have an ignited and radiant soul?

Your "utmost desire must be to confer happiness upon each other," said 'Abdu'l-Bahá (p. 138). What are some ways you can bring happiness to the people in your life?

Chapter 23: Bahá'í Marriage

The Bahá'í marriage vow is "We will all, verily, abide by the Will of God." This is different from traditional wedding vows. What might it look like when you abide by God's will?

'Abdu'l-Bahá encouraged interracial marriage between Louis and Louisa Gregory, saying it was "a good way to efface racial differences" (p. 147). What are some ways an interracial marriage can help build race unity?

Chapter 24: A Delightful Spot

Sarah Farmer established Green Acre so people's minds and souls could be refreshed by learning and nature. How does being in nature impact you? How do you feel when you learn something new?

'Abdu'l-Bahá said "We must consider everyone as related to us. . . ." (p. 152). What are some ways you can treat people like members of your family?

"A good Jew can also become a Bahá'í. The truth of the religion of Moses and Bahá'u'lláh is one," said 'Abdu'l-Bahá (p. 153). What does that mean to you?

Chapter 25: Fred's Ride

Fred Mortenson said the Word of God changed his character and "made me a living soul" (p. 156). How does the Word of God influence you?

Fred put his negative choices behind him and changed his life. What have you learned from mistakes or unwise choices you've made?

Chapter 26: In Montreal

'Abdu'l-Bahá said, "look at Me, follow Me, be as I am" (p. 162). What are ways we can try to be similar to 'Abdu'l-Bahá?

When a person is detached, he is capable of "revolutionizing the whole world," said 'Abdu'l-Bahá (p. 164). What does it mean to be detached? Why do you think that virtue is powerful?

Chapter 27: A Home Becomes a Shrine

'Abdu'l-Bahá urged us to be grateful in times of want and trouble (p. 169). What might that look like?

Have you ever had a negative experience that also brought some blessings? What are some examples?

Chapter 28: The Journey West

'Abdu'l-Bahá said, "in the path of God we must regard troubles as blessings and discomforts as greatest bounties" (p. 173). How might it feel to think about troubles and discomforts in this way?

'Abdu'l-Bahá said that Bahá'u'lláh's spiritual aid was vital for His successful journey. Are there times you've felt the power of divine assistance? What was that like?

Chapter 29: Unique One of the Orient
"All war and conflict, bloodshed and battle . . . has been due to some form of prejudice. . . . " said 'Abdu'l-Bahá (p. 182). Why do you think prejudice leads to conflict?

'Abdu'l-Bahá said, "Religion becomes the cause of love in human hearts" (p. 182). What are some ways that religion can lead to love and unity?

Chapter 30: At the Home of Science
'Abdu'l-Bahá said that science is "the greatest attainment in the world of humanity" (p. 186). What are some ways that science assists the world?

The Bahá'í Faith teaches that science and religion agree and both help us to make discoveries. How might looking at science and religion this way help the world?

Chapter 31: Unity among Religions
'Abdu'l-Bahá urged Jewish people to accept Christ and Muhammad (p. 192). Afterward, the Christians and Jews visited each other and gave talks about unity. Why do you think interfaith activities can have a powerful influence on people?

What are some ways you can help to encourage unity among people from different religions?

Chapter 32: A Firm Believer

"Are you happy?" is a question that 'Abdu'l-Bahá often asked. What impact might this question have on people?

What can help you focus on happiness instead of life's difficulties?

Chapter 33: Gatherings of Unity

'Abdu'l-Bahá encouraged us to be "confident and steadfast" because God helps souls whose "aim is to serve humanity" (p. 206). What does it mean to be confident? What does steadfastness look like?

Because black people weren't welcome at a New York hotel, the black friends were invited to a banquet in a private home where the white women served them (p. 207). How might that experience have impacted each group?

Chapter 34: Become Brilliant Lamps

'Abdu'l-Bahá said, "the obstacle to human happiness is racial or religious prejudice" (p. 211). How does prejudice lead to unhappiness?

What are some things you can do to help eliminate racial and religious prejudice?

Notes

Introduction

1. Allen L. Ward, *239 Days: 'Abdu'l-Bahá's Journey in America,* pp. 16, 17, 85.

2. Shoghi Effendi, *God Passes By,* p. 290.

3. Howard Colby Ives, *Portals to Freedom,* p. 29.

4. Juliet Thompson, *The Diary of Juliet Thompson,* pp. 313, 273.

5. *Portals to Freedom,* p. 32.

6. Ibid., p. 127.

7. Ibid., p. 49.

8. Maḥmúd-i-Zarqání, *Maḥmúd's Diary,* p. 290.

9. 'Abdu'l-Bahá, *The Promulgation of Universal Peace,* pp. 4, 3.

Chapter 1

1. 'Abdu'l-Bahá, *'Abdu'l-Bahá in London,* p. 120.

2. Wendell Phillips Dodge, "'Abdu'l-Bahá's Arrival in America," *Star of the West* 3, no. 3 (28 April 1912): pp. 3-5.

3. Juliet Thompson, *The Diary of Juliet Thompson,* pp. 232-34.

4. O. Z. Whitehead and Marzieh Gail, "Marjory," *World Order,* Summer 1973, p. 48.

Chapter 2

1. 'Abdu'l-Bahá, *The Promulgation of Universal Peace,* pp. 3-4.
2. Howard Colby Ives, *Portals to Freedom,* p. 36.
3. Ibid., pp. 26-33.
4. Ibid., pp. 40, 69.
5. Ibid., pp. 122, 123.
6. Ibid., pp. 197-98.
7. Ibid., p. 143.

Chapter 3

1. "Called W. K. Lathrop a Liar: George Bradish's Fiery Speech at a Church Meeting," *The New York Times* (11 May 1893): n.p.
2. Juliet Thompson, *The Diary of Juliet Thompson,* p. 227.
3. Wendell Phillips Dodge, "'Abdu'l-Bahá's Arrival in America," *Star of the West* 3, no. 3 (28 April 1912): p. 5.
4. 'Abdu'l-Bahá, *The Promulgation of Universal Peace,* pp. 14–17.
5.'Abdu'l-Bahá, quoted in Ward, *239 Days: 'Abdu'l-Bahá's Journey in America,* p. 23.
6. Maḥmúd-i-Zarqání, *Maḥmúd's Diary,* pp. 44-45.

Chapter 4

1. Juliet Thompson, *The Diary of Juliet Thompson,* pp. 255-56.
2. Ibid., p. 255.
3. Ibid., p. 281.

4. Ibid., p. 251.

5. 'Abdu'l-Bahá, *The Promulgation of Universal Peace*, pp. 44–46.

6. Juliet Thompson, *The Diary of Juliet Thompson*, p. 260.

7. Ibid., pp. 252, 266.

Chapter 5

1. Howard Colby Ives, *Portals to Freedom*, pp. 63-67.

Chapter 6

1. Marzieh Gail, "'Abdu'l-Bahá: Portrayals from East and West: Materials from the Papers of Ali-Kuli Khan and the Conversations of John and Louise Bosch," in *Dawn over Mount Hira and Other Essays*, p. 204.

2. 'Abdu'l-Bahá, quoted in ibid., p. 205.

3. Ibid., pp. 207-208.

4. John Bosch, quoted in ibid., pp. 208-209.

5. 'Abdu'l-Bahá, quoted in ibid., p. 205.

Chapter 7

1. Louis G. Gregory, quoted in Morrison, *To Move the World*, p. 16.

2. 'Abdu'l-Bahá, quoted in ibid., p. 7.

3. Louis G. Gregory, "Some Recollections of the Early Days of the Bahá'í Faith in Washington, DC," Louis G. Gregory Papers, National Bahá'í Archives, Wilmette, Illinois.

4. Louis G. Gregory, *Race Unity*, "Chapter XVIII: Reminiscent," unpublished manuscript. Louis G. Gregory Papers, National Bahá'í Archives, Wilmette, Illinois.

5. 'Abdu'l-Bahá, quoted in Morrison, *To Move the World*, p. 45.

6. Louis G. Gregory, quoted in ibid., p. 86.

7. Allan L. Ward, *239 Days: 'Abdu'l-Bahá's Journey in America*, p. 40.

8. 'Abdu'l-Bahá, *The Promulgation of Universal Peace*, pp. 60–63.

9. Louis G. Gregory, "Racial Amity in America: An Historical Review," in *The Bahá'í World: A Biennial International Record, Volume VII, 1936-1938*, pp. 654–55.

10. Louis G. Gregory, "Some Recollections of the Early Days of the Bahá'í Faith in Washington, DC," Louis G. Gregory Papers, National Bahá'í Archives, Wilmette, Illinois.

Chapter 8

1. Marzieh Gail, *Summon Up Remembrance*, p. 65.

2. Ibid., p. 98.

3. Ibid., p. 100.

4. Marzieh Gail, *Summon Up Remembrance*, p. 109.

5. Ibid., p. 147.

6. 'Abdu'l-Bahá, quoted in Bagdadi, "'Abdu'l-Bahá in America: Chapter II—Washington, D.C." *Star of the West* 19, no. 3 (June 1928): p. 90.

7. Harlan Ober, "Louis G. Gregory," in *The Bahá'í World: A Biennial International Record, Volume XII, 1950-1954*, pp. 668-69.

8. 'Abdu'l-Bahá, quoted in Bagdadi, "'Abdu'l-Bahá in America: Chapter II—Washington, D.C," *Star of the West* 19, no. 3 (June 1928): p. 89.

9. Louis G. Gregory, quoted in Morrison, *To Move the World*, p. 53.

NOTES

Chapter 9

1. O. Z. Whitehead, *Some Bahá'ís to Remember*, pp. 76-77.

2. 'Abdu'l-Bahá, quoted in ibid., p. 79.

3. 'Abdu'l-Bahá, quoted in Bagdadi, "'Abdu'l-Bahá in America: Chapter II—Washington, D.C.," *Star of the West* 19, no. 3 (June 1928): p. 90.

4. Commander Lightoller, "Titanic," in *The Story of the* Titanic *as Told by Its Survivors*, pp. 280, 282.

5. 'Abdu'l-Bahá, quoted in Zarqání, *Mahmud's Diary*, p. 10.

6. 'Abdu'l-Bahá, *The Promulgation of Universal Peace*, pp. 63–65.

7. Juliet Thompson, *The Diary of Juliet Thompson*, pp. 273-74.

8. Mahmúd-i-Zarqání, *Mahmud's Diary*, p. 218.

Chapter 10

1. 'Abdu'l-Bahá, quoted in Parsons, *Abdu'l-Bahá in America: Agnes Parsons' Diary*, ed. Richard Hollinger , p. 93.

2. Marzieh Gail, *Arches of the Years*, p. 82.

3. Ibid., p. 80.

4. Ibid., p. 82

5. Ibid., p. 80.

6. Ibid., p. 82.

7. Joseph H. Hannen, "'Abdu'l-Bahá in Washington, D.C.," *Star of the West* 3, no. 3 (28 April 1912): p. 7.

8. 'Abdu'l-Bahá, quoted in Bagdadi, "'Abdu'l-Bahá in America: Chapter II—Washington, D.C.," *Star of the West* 19, no. 3 (June 1928): p. 89.

9. 'Abdu'l-Bahá, *The Promulgation of Universal Peace*, pp. 71–73.

10. Marzieh Gail, *Arches of the Years*, p. 85.

11. Agnes Parsons, *Abdu'l-Bahá in America*, ed. Richard Hollinger, pp. 41, 43.

Chapter 11

1. Maḥmúd-i-Zarqání, *Mahmud's Diary*, p. 58.

2. Shoghi Effendi, *God Passes By*, p. 293.

3. Ibid.

4. Ibid., pp. 293–94.

5. Ḍíyá Pá<u>sh</u>á, quoted in Zarqání, *Mahmúd's Diary*, p. 60.

6. 'Abdu'l-Bahá, quoted in Bagdadi, "'Abdu'l-Bahá in America: Chapter II—Washington, D.C.," *Star of the West* 19, no. 3 (June 1928): pp. 90-91.

7. Juliet Thompson, *The Diary of Juliet Thompson*, p. 276.

8. 'Abdu'l-Bahá, quoted in Zarqání, *Mahmúd's Diary*, p. 66.

Chapter 12

1. 'Abdu'l-Bahá, quoted in Bagdadi, "'Abdu'l-Bahá in America: Chapter III—Chicago, Ill." *Star of the West* 19, no. 4 (July 1928): p. 111.

2. Bahá'u'lláh, quoted in Whitmore, *The Dawning Place: The Building of the Temple*, p. 10.

3. 'Abdu'l-Bahá, quoted in Rutstein, *Corinne True: Faithful Handmaid of 'Abdu'l-Bahá*, p. 27.

4. Ibid., p. 28.

5. Ibid., pp. 40–41.

6. Ibid., p. 41.

7. Corinne True, quoted in Whitmore, *The Dawning Place: The Building of the Temple*, p. 29.

8. 'Abdu'l-Bahá, quoted in Kempton, "Corinne Knight True," *The Bahá'í World: An International Record, Volume XIII, 1954-1963*, p. 847.

9. 'Abdu'l-Bahá, quoted in *The Bahá'í World: An International Record, Volume XIII, 1954-1963*, p. 847.

10. Moses True, quoted in *Corinne True*, p. 87.

11. 'Abdu'l-Bahá, quoted in ibid., p. 99.

12. 'Abdu'l-Bahá, *The Promulgation of Universal Peace*, pp. 90-92.

13. Zia Bagdadi, "'Abdu'l-Bahá in America: Chapter III—Chicago, Ill." *Star of the West* 19, no. 4 (July 1928): p. 113.

Chapter 13

1. Albert R. Windust, "Mrs. Esther Tobin: 1863-1944," *The Bahá'í World: A Biennial International Record, Volume X, 1944-1946*, pp. 543-44.

2. Bruce W. Whitmore, *The Dawning Place: The Building of the Temple*, pp. 42-48.

3. Psalms 118:22.

4. 'Abdu'l-Bahá, *The Promulgation of Universal Peace*, pp. 97-98.

5. 'Abdu'l-Bahá, quoted in Whitmore, *The Dawning Place: The Building of the Temple*, p. 65.

Chapter 14

1. Zia Bagdadi, "Chicago, Ill.," *Star of the West* 19, no. 4 (July 1928): p. 114.

2. 'Abdu'l-Bahá, *The Promulgation of Universal Peace*, pp. 126-27.

3. Ibid., p. 128.

4. Maḥmúd-i-Zarqání, *Mahmud's Diary*, p. 85.

5. 'Abdu'l-Bahá, quoted in Bagdadi, "'Abdu'l-Bahá in America," *Star of the West* 19, no. 5 (August 1928): pp. 140-141.

Chapter 15

1. Zia M. Bagdadi, *Treasures of the East: The Life of Nine Oriental Countries*, pp. 81-82.

2. 'Abdu'l-Bahá, *The Promulgation of Universal Peace*, p. 662.

3. Maḥmúd-i-Zarqání, *Mahmud's Diary*, p. 101.

4. Zia Bagdadi, "'Abdu'l-Bahá in America," *Star of the West* 19, no. 6 (September 1928), pp. 180-82.

Chapter 16

1. Elizabeth Frost and Kathryn Cullen-DuPont, *Women's Suffrage in America: An Eyewitness History*, pp. 287-303; "The Triangle Factory Fire," http://www.ilr.cornell.edu/trianglefire/narrative1.html.

2. Elizabeth Frost and Kathryn Cullen-DuPont, *Women's Suffrage in America*, pp. 268, 272, 294.

3. 'Abdu'l-Bahá, quoted in Dodge, "'Abdu'l-Bahá's Arrival in America," *Star of the West* 3, no. 3 (28 April 1912): p. 4.

4. "Addresses Delivered by Abdul-Baha in New York and Vicinity," *Star of the West* 3, no. 8 (August 1, 1912): pp. 15, 18.

5. 'Abdu'l-Bahá, *The Promulgation of Universal Peace*, pp. 184-89.

6. Maḥmúd-i-Zarqání, *Mahmud's Diary*, p. 106.

7. 'Abdu'l-Bahá, *The Promulgation of Universal Peace*, p. 529.

Chapter 17

1. O. Z. Whitehead, *Some Early Bahá'ís of the West*, pp. 75-76.

2. Maḥmúd-i-Zarqání, *Mahmud's Diary*, p. 107.

3. 'Abdu'l-Bahá, quoted in Bagdadi, "'Abdu'l-Bahá in America," *Star of the West* 19, no. 6 (September 1928): p. 183.

4. Abdu'l-Bahá, *The Promulgation of Universal Peace*, pp. 184-89.

5. Maḥmúd-i-Zarqání, *Mahmud's Diary*, p. 110.

6. Marzieh Gail, *Arches of the Years*, p. 91.

Chapter 18

1. Juliet Thompson, *The Diary of Juliet Thompson*, p. 278.

2. Ibid., p. 298–99.

3. Ibid., p. 308.

4. Ibid., pp. 302–303.

5. Ibid., pp. 311, 313.

6. Ibid., p. 311.

7. Ibid., p. 375.

8. Ibid., p. 389.

9. Marzieh Gail, "At 48 West Tenth," preface to *The Diary of Juliet Thompson*, p. xix.

10. Juliet Thompson, *The Diary of Juliet Thompson*, p. 390.

Chapter 19

1. 'Abdu'l-Bahá, *The Promulgation of Universal Peace*, pp. 270–71.

Chapter 20

1. 'Abdu'l-Bahá, quoted in J. G. Grundy and H. MacNutt, "Taking of the Moving Picture of Abdul-Baha, the Centre of the Covenant," *Star of the West* 3, no. 10 (8 September 1912): p. 3.

2. Howard MacNutt, quoted in Whitehead, *Some Early Bahá'ís of the West*, p. 38.

3. 'Abdu'l-Bahá, quoted in Zarqání, *Maḥmud's Diary*, pp. 135–36.

4. Ibid., p. 136–37.

5. J. G. Grundy and H. MacNutt, "Taking of the Moving Picture of Abdul-Baha, the Centre of the Covenant," *Star of the West* 3, no. 10 (8 September 1912): p. 3.

6. Ibid., p. 4.

7. National Spiritual Assembly of the Bahá'ís of the United States, To all Local Spiritual Assemblies and Registered Bahá'í Groups, September 23, 2008.

8. 'Abdu'l-Bahá, quoted in Whitehead, *Some Early Bahá'ís of the West*, p. 41.

Chapter 21

1. In a book called the Kitáb-i-Aqdas (the Most Holy Book), Bahá'u'lláh gives 'Abdu'l-Bahá the authority to interpret His writings.

2. Juliet Thompson, *The Diary of Juliet Thompson*, pp. 311–14.

3. 'Abdu'l-Bahá, quoted in Ruhe-Schoen, *A Love Which Does Not Wait*, p. 8.

4. 'Abdu'l-Bahá, quoted in Metelmann, *Lua Getsinger: Herald of the Covenant*, pp. 68–69.

5. Stanwood Cobb, "Memories of 'Abdu'l-Bahá," in *In His Presence: Visits to 'Abdu'l-Bahá, Memoirs of Roy Wilhelm, Stanwood Cobb, Genevieve L. Coy*, p. 35.

6. Lua Getsinger, quoted in *Portals to Freedom*, p. 85.

7. See Chapter 13.

8. 'Abdu'l-Bahá, quoted in "'The Covenant' and 'The Center of the Covenant," *Star of the West* 5, no. 15 (12 December 1914): pp. 227–228; Metelmann, *Lua Getsinger*, p. 157.

9. Juliet Thompson, *The Diary of Juliet Thompson*, pp. 323–25.

Chapter 22

1. 'Abdu'l-Bahá, *The Promulgation of Universal Peace*, p. 289.

2. 'Abdu'l-Bahá, quoted in Holley, "Roy Wilhelm," *The Bahá'í World: A Biennial International Record*, Volume XII, 1950-1954, p. 664.

3. Roy Wilhelm, "Knock, and It Shall Be Opened Unto You," in *In His Presence*, pp. 7–8.

4. Ibid., p. 13.

5. Ibid., pp. 16–17.

6. Maḥmúd-i-Zarqání, *Maḥmud's Diary*, p. 150.

7. Juliet Thompson, *The Diary of Juliet Thompson*, p. 322.

8. 'Abdu'l-Bahá, *The Promulgation of Universal Peace*, pp. 298–300.

9. Maḥmúd-i-Zarqání, *Maḥmud's Diary*, p. 151.

10. Juliet Thompson, *The Diary of Juliet Thompson*, pp. 324–25.

11. 'Abdu'l-Bahá, "Tablet Revealed by Abdul-Baha to Mr. Roy C. Wilhelm," *Star of the West* 4, no. 14 (23 November 1913): p. 240.

Chapter 23

1. Mabel Rice-Wray Ives, "Grace Robarts Ober," *The Bahá'í World: A Biennial International Record, Volume VIII*, p. 658.

2. 'Abdu'l-Bahá, "To Mr. And Mrs. Harlan F. Ober," *Star of the West* 7, no. 17 (19 January 1917): p. 167.

3. Mabel Rice-Wray Ives, "Grace Robarts Ober," *The Bahá'í World: A Biennial International Record, Volume VIII*, p. 658.

4. Lua Getsinger, quoted in Whitehead, *Some Bahá'ís to Remember*, p. 120.

5. Harlan Ober, quoted in ibid., p. 121.

6. Harlan Ober, quoted in "Harlan Foster Ober: 1881-1962," *The Bahá'í World: A Biennial International Record, Volume XIII*, p. 868.

7. 'Abdu'l-Bahá, quoted in "Harlan Foster Ober: 1881-1962," *The Bahá'í World: A Biennial International Record, Volume XIII*, p. 869.

8. Ibid.

9. Juliet Thompson, *The Diary of Juliet Thompson*, pp. 350–351.

10. Annie T. Boylan, "Matrimony in the Bahá'í Spirit," *Star of the West* 3, no. 12 (16 October 1912): p. 14.

11. 'Abdu'l-Bahá, *Bahá'í Prayers*, p. 120.

12. 'Abdu'l-Bahá, quoted in *Star of the West* 3, no. 12 (16 October 1912): p. 15.

13. 'Abdu'l-Bahá, quoted in Zarqání, *Maḥmud's Diary*, p. 172.

14. Mabel Rice-Wray Ives, "Grace Robarts Ober," *The Bahá'í World: A Biennial International Record, Volume VIII*, p. 658.

15. 'Abdu'l-Bahá, "To Mr. and Mrs. Harlan F. Ober," *Star of the West* 7, no. 17 (19 January 1917): p. 167.

16. 'Abdu'l-Bahá, quoted in Morrison, *To Move the World*, p. 45.

17. 'Abdu'l-Bahá, quoted ibid., p. 45.

18. Louis Gregory, quoted in ibid., p. 71.

19. 'Abdu'l-Bahá, quoted in ibid., p. 72.

Chapter 24

1. Sarah Farmer, quoted in Atkinson, et al., *Green Acre on the Piscataqua*, p. 47.

2. Ibid., p. 13.

3. Quoted in ibid., p. 30.

4. Ibid., p. 34.

5. 'Abdu'l-Bahá, quoted in ibid., p. 39.

6. 'Abdu'l-Bahá, *The Promulgation of Universal Peace*, p. 364.

7. Ibid., pp. 369–77.

8. 'Abdu'l-Bahá, quoted in Atkinson, et al., *Green Acre on the Piscataqua*, p. 53.

9. 'Abdu'l-Bahá, quoted in Zarqání, *Maḥmud's Diary*, p. 215.

10. Ibid., p. 216.

11. Ibid., pp. 219–20.

Chapter 25

1. Fred Mortensen, "When a Soul Meets the Master," *Star of the West* 14, no. 12 (March 1924): p. 366.

2. Ibid.

3. Ibid.

4. Juliet Thompson, *The Diary of Juliet Thompson*, p. 359.

5. Fred Mortensen, "When a Soul Meets the Master," *Star of the West* 14, no. 12 (March 1924), p. 367.

6. 'Abdu'l-Bahá, quoted in "Fred Mortensen," *The Bahá'í World: A Biennial International Record, Volume XI, 1946–1950*, p. 486.

Chapter 26

1. Maḥmúd-i-Zarqání, *Maḥmud's Diary*, p. 227.

2. Janet Ruhe-Schoen, *A Love Which Does Not Wait*, pp. 35–36.

3. Marion Holley, "May Ellis Maxwell," *The Bahá'í World: A Biennial International Record, Volume VIII*, p. 633.

4. 'Abdu'l-Bahá, quoted in Ruhe-Schoen, p. 38.

5. Ibid., pp. 41–42.

6. Amatu'l-Bahá Rúḥíyyih Khánum, quoted in ibid, p. 44.

7. Janet Ruhe-Schoen, *A Love Which Does Not Wait*, p. 49.

8. Maḥmúd-i-Zarqání, *Maḥmud's Diary*, p. 247.

9. 'Abdu'l-Bahá, quoted in Hoonaard, *The Origins of the Bahá'í Community of Canada, 1898–1949* p. 46.

10. 'Abdu'l-Bahá, quoted in Zarqání, *Maḥmud's Diary*, p. 228.

11. Maḥmúd-i-Zarqání, *Maḥmud's Diary*, pp. 230–231.

12. 'Abdu'l-Bahá, *The Promulgation of Universal Peace*, pp. 413–20.

Chapter 27

1. 'Abdu'l-Bahá, *The Promulgation of Universal Peace*, pp. 420–24.

2. 'Abdu'l-Bahá, quoted in *Maḥmud's Diary*, p. 244.

3. Ibid., p. 238.

4. Ibid., pp. 237, 239.

5. Ibid., p. 243.

6. 'Abdu'l-Bahá, quoted in Violette Na<u>kh</u>javání, *A Tribute to Amatu'l-Bahá Rúhíyyih <u>Kh</u>ánum,* pp. 4–5, 3.

7. 'Abdu'l-Bahá, quoted in Zarqání, *Mahmud's Diary,* p. 247.

8. 'Abdu'l-Bahá, quoted in van den Hoonard, *The Origins of the Bahá'í Community of Canada, 1898–1949,* p. 53.

9. 'Abdu'l-Bahá, quoted in Na<u>kh</u>javání, *A Tribute to Amatu'l-Bahá Rúhíyyih <u>Kh</u>ánum,* p. 11.

10. May Maxwell, quoted in ibid., p. 7.

11. 'Abdu'l-Bahá, quoted in *Mahmud's Diary,* p. 249.

12. Amatu'l-Bahá Rúhíyyih <u>Kh</u>ánum, quoted in "The Bahá'í Shrine in Canada," http://www.ca.bahai.org/shrine.

Chapter 28

1. 'Abdu'l-Bahá, quoted in Zarqání, *Mahmud's Diary,* pp. 247–48.

2. Ibid., p. 251.

3. Mahmúd-i-Zarqání, *Mahmud's Diary,* p. 292.

4. 'Abdu'l-Bahá, quoted in ibid., pp. 292–93.

5. Mahmúd-i-Zarqání, *Mahmud's Diary,* p. 294.

6. 'Abdu'l-Bahá, quoted in ibid., p. 294.

7. Mahmúd-i-Zarqání, *Mahmud's Diary,* p. 299.

8. 'Abdu'l-Bahá, quoted in ibid., p. 304.

9. Mahmúd-i-Zarqání, *Mahmud's Diary,* p. 302.

10. Ramona Allen Brown, *Memories of 'Abdu'l-Bahá: Recollections of the Early Days of the Bahá'í Faith in California,* pp. 4–6.

11. Ibid., pp. 35–37.

Chapter 29

1. 'Abdu'l-Bahá, quoted in Zarqání, *Mahmud's Diary*, p. 304.

2. O. Z. Whitehead, *Some Bahá'ís to Remember*, p. 179.

3. 'Abdu'l-Bahá, quoted in ibid., p. 181.

4. Kanichi Yamamoto, quoted in ibid., p. 182.

5. Frances Orr Allen, "Abdul-Baha in San Francisco, California," *Star of the West* 3, no. 12 (16 October 1912): p. 9.

6. 'Abdu'l-Bahá, *The Promulgation of Universal Peace*, pp. 485–92.

7. 'Abdu'l-Bahá, quoted in Allen, *Star of the West* 3, no. 12 (16 October 1912): p. 9.

8. 'Abdu'l-Bahá, quoted in Zarqání, *Mahmud's Diary*, p. 325.

Chapter 30

1. Lua Getsiner, quoted in Metelmann, *Lua Getsinger: Herald of the Covenant*, pp. 176, 177.

2. David Starr Jordan, quoted in "Address by Abdul-Baha at Leland Stanford Junior University, Palo Alto, California," *Star of the West* 3, no. 12 (16 October 1912): p. 10.

3. 'Abdu'l-Bahá, *The Promulgation of Universal Peace*, pp. 492–502.

4. Mahmúd-i-Zarqání, *Mahmud's Diary*, p. 311.

5. "Abdul-Baha, the Bahai Prophet, Speaks at Stanford University," from *The Palo Altan*, in *Star of the West* 3, no. 13 (Nov. 4, 1912): p. 13.

6. 'Abdu'l-Bahá, "Tablet to the Editor of 'The Palo Altan,'" *Star of the West* 3, no. 13 (4 November 1912): p. 8.

7. Lua Getsinger, quoted in Metelmann, *Lua Getsinger: Herald of the Covenant,* p. 179.

Chapter 31

1. Maḥmúd-i-Zarqání, *Maḥmud's Diary,* p. 315–16.

2. Rabbi Martin Meyer, quoted in "Message to the Jews," *Star of the West* 3, no. 13 (4 November 1912): p. 3.

3. Ramona Allen Brown, *Memories of 'Abdu'l-Bahá,* p. 49.

4. 'Abdu'l-Bahá, *The Promulgation of Universal Peace,* pp. 510–23.

5. 'Abdu'l-Bahá, quoted in Zarqání, *Maḥmud's Diary,* p. 325.

6. Maḥmúd-i-Zarqání, *Maḥmud's Diary,* p. 325.

7. Frances Orr Allen, *Star of the West* 3, no. 13 (4 November 1912): p. 11.

8. Ibid., p. 12.

9. 'Abdu'l-Bahá, quoted in Zarqání, *Maḥmud's Diary,* p. 336.

10. Ibid., p. 332.

Chapter 32

1. 'Abdu'l-Bahá, quoted in Robert H. Stockman, *Thornton Chase: The First American Bahá'í,* p. 252.

2. Ibid., p. 148.

3. Thornton Chase, *In Galilee,* pp. 27, 29–30.

4. Ibid, pp. 34–35.

5. Ibid., p. 39.

6. 'Abdu'l-Bahá, quoted in Chase, *In Galilee,* p. 40.

7. 'Abdu'l-Bahá, quoted in *Thornton Chase: The First American Bahá'í,* p. 211.

8. Ibid., pp. 227–28.

9. Thornton Chase, quoted in ibid., pp. 248–49.

10. 'Abdu'l-Bahá, quoted in Zarqání, *Mahmud's Diary*, p. 336.

11. Mirza Ahmad Sohrab, "Abdul-Baha at the Grave of Thornton Chase," *Star of the West* 3, no. 13 (4 November 1912): p. 15.

12. 'Abdu'l-Bahá, quoted in Zarqání, *Mahmud's Diary*, pp. 348–49.

Chapter 33

1. 'Abdu'l-Bahá, *The Promulgation of Universal Peace*, pp. 630–32.

2. Juliet Thompson, *The Diary of Juliet Thompson*, p. 376.

3. Mahmúd-i-Zarqání, *Mahmud's Diary*, p. 406.

4. Ibid., pp. 406–407.

5. 'Abdu'l-Bahá, quoted in ibid., p. 407.

6. Ibid., pp. 407–408.

Chapter 34

1. 'Abdu'l-Bahá, quoted in Zarqání, *Mahmud's Diary*, pp. 414–15.

2. Ibid., p. 415.

3. Mahmúd-i-Zarqání, *Mahmud's Diary*, p. 429.

4. 'Abdu'l-Bahá, *The Promulgation of Universal Peace*, pp. 660–63.

Bibliography

Works by 'Abdu'l-Bahá

'Abdu'l-Bahá in London. London: Bahá'í Publishing Trust, 1987.

The Promulgation of Universal Peace: Talks Delivered by 'Abdu'l-Bahá during His Visit to the United States and Canada in 1912, new ed. Comp. Howard MacNutt. Wilmette: Bahá'í Publishing Trust, 2007.

Works by Shoghi Effendi

God Passes By. Wilmette, IL: Bahá'í Publishing Trust, 1974.

Bahá'í Compilations

Bahá'í Prayers: A Selection of Prayers Revealed by Bahá'u'lláh, the Báb, and 'Abdu'l-Bahá. Wilmette, IL: Bahá'í Publishing Trust, 2002.

Bahá'í History

"Abdul-Baha with the Children of the Friends in Chicago," from notes by Ella Goodall Cooper and Ella M. Bailey, *Star of the West* 3, no. 7 (13 July 1912), pp. 6–7.

"Abdul-Baha, the Bahai Prophet, Speaks at Stanford University," from *The Palo Altan,* in *Star of the West* 3, no. 13 (4 November 1912), pp. 13–14.

"Address by Abdul-Baha at Leland Stanford Junior University, Palo Alto, California," *Star of the West* 3, no. 12 (16 October 1912), pp. 10–14.

"Addresses Delivered by Abdul-Baha in New York and Vicinity," *Star of the West* 3, no. 8 (1 August 1912), pp. 3–15, 18–22.

'Abdu'l-Bahá. "Tablet to the Editor of 'The Palo Altan,'" *Star of the West* 3, no. 13 (4 November 1912), p. 8.

_____ . "To Mr. And Mrs. Harlan F. Ober," *Star of the West* 7, no. 17 (19 January 1917), p. 167.

_____ . "Tablet Revealed by Abdul-Baha to Mr. Roy C. Wilhelm," *Star of the West* 4, no. 14 (23 November 1913), p. 240.

Mírzá Ahmad Sohrab, "Abdul-Baha at the Grave of Thornton Chase," *Star of the West* 3, no. 13 (4 November 1912), pp. 14–15.

Allen, Frances Orr. "Abdul-Baha in San Francisco, California," *Star of the West* 3, no. 12 (16 October 1912), pp. 9–10.

Atkinson, Anne Gordon, Robert Atkinson, Rosanne Buzzell, Richard Grover, Diane Iverson, Robert H. Stockman, Burton W. F. Trafton, Jr. *Green Acre on the Piscataqua: A Centennial*

Celebration. Eliot, ME: Green Acre Bahá'í School Council, 1991.

Bagdadi, Zia. "'Abdu'l-Bahá in America: Chapter II—Washington, D.C." *Star of the West* 19, no. 3 (June 1928), pp. 87–92.

_____. "'Abdu'l-Bahá in America: Chapter III—Chicago, Ill." *Star of the West* 19,no. 4 (July 1928), pp. 111–15.

_____. 'Abdu'l-Bahá in America," *Star of the West* 19, no. 5 (August 1928), pp. 140-44.

_____. "'Abdu'l-Bahá in America," *Star of the West* 19, no. 6 (September 1928), pp. 180–85.

_____. *Treasures of the East: The Life of Nine Oriental Countries*. Chicago: 1930.

The Bahá'í Community of Canada. "The Bahá'í Shrine in Canada." http://www.ca.bahai.org/shrine.

Balyuzi, H.M. *'Abdu'l-Bahá: The Centre of the Covenant of Bahá'u'lláh.* Oxford: George Ronald, 1987.

Boylan, Annie T. "Matrimony in the Bahá'í Spirit," *Star of the West* 3, no. 12 (16 October 1912), pp. 14–15.

Brown, Ramona Allen. *Memories of 'Abdu'l-Bahá: Recollections of the Early Days of the Bahá'í Faith in California*. Wilmette, IL: Bahá'í Publishing Trust, 1980.

Chase, Thornton. *In Galilee*. Los Angeles: Kalimát, 1985.

Cobb, Stanwood. "Memories of 'Abdu'l-Bahá," in *In His Presence: Visits to 'Abdu'l-Bahá, Memoirs of Roy Wilhelm, Stanwood Cobb, Genevieve L. Coy.* Los Angeles: Kalimát, 1989, pp. 25–64.

"The Covenant" and "The Center of the Covenant," *Star of the West* 5, no. 15 (12 December 1914), pp. 227–28.

Dodge, Wendell Phillips, "'Abdu'l-Bahá's Arrival in America," *Star of the West* 3, no. 3 (28 April 1912), pp. 3–5.

Earl, Joy Hill, "Louisa Mathew Gregory, 1866–1956." *The Bahá'í World: An International Record, Volume XIII, 1954–1963,* comp. Prepared under the supervision of The Universal House of Justice. Haifa: The Universal House of Justice, 1970, pp. 876–878.

"Fred Mortensen," *The Bahá'í World: A Biennial International Record, Volume XI, 1946–1950,* comp. Prepared under the supervision of the National Spiritual Assembly of the Bahá'ís of the United States and Canada with the approval of Shoghi Effendi. Wilmette, IL: Bahá'í Publishing Trust, 1928, pp. 483–86.

Gail, Marzieh. "'Abdu'l-Bahá: Portrayals from East and West: Materials from the Papers of Ali-Kuli Khan and the Conversations of John and Louise Bosch," in *Dawn over Mount Hira and Other Essays.* Oxford: George Ronald, 1976, pp. 194–216.

_____. "'Abdu'l-Bahá in America," in *Dawn Over Mount Hira and Other Essays.* Oxford: George Ronald, 1976, 184-93.

_____. *Arches of the Years.* Oxford: George Ronald, 1991.

_____. "At 48 West Tenth," preface to *The Diary of Juliet Thompson* (Los Angeles: Kalimat, 1983), pp. xviii–xix.

_____. *Summon Up Remembrance.* Oxford: George Ronald, 1987.

Green Acre Bahá'í School and the Portsmouth Peace Treaty. http://portsmouthpeacetreaty.org/BahaCenter_treaty.cfm.

Gregory, Louis G. "Some Recollections of the Early Days of the Bahá'í Faith in Washington, DC." Louis G. Gregory Papers, National Bahá'í Archives, Wilmette, Illinois.

_____. *Race Unity,* "Chapter XVIII: Reminiscent," unpublished manuscript. Louis G. Gregory Papers, National Bahá'í Archives, Wilmette, Illinois.

_____. "Racial Amity in America: An Historical Review." *The Bahá'í World: A Biennial International Record, Volume VII, 1936-1938,* comp. Prepared under the supervision of the National Spiritual Assembly of the Bahá'ís of the United States and Canada with the approval of Shoghi Effendi. Wilmette, IL: Bahá'í Publishing Trust, 1939, pp. 652–66.

Grundy, J. G. Grundy and H. MacNutt. "Taking of the Moving Picture of Abdul-Baha, the Centre of the Covenant," *Star of the West* 3, no. 10 (8 September 1912), pp. 3–4.

Hannen, Joseph H. "'Abdu'l-Bahá in Washington, D.C." *Star of the West,* 3, no. 3 (28 April 1912), pp. 6–24.

Holley, Horace. "Roy Wilhelm." *The Bahá'í World: A Biennial International Record, Volume XII, 1950-1954,* comp. Prepared under the supervision of the National Spiritual Assembly of the Bahá'ís of the United States and Canada with the approval of Shoghi Effendi. Wilmette, IL: Bahá'í Publishing Trust, 1956, pp. 662–64.

Holley, Marion. "May Ellis Maxwell," *The Bahá'í World, Volume VIII, 1938–1940,* comp. Prepared under the supervision of the National Spiritual Assembly of the Bahá'ís of the United States and Canada with the approval of Shoghi Effendi. Wilmette, IL: Bahá'í Publishing Trust, 1942, pp. 631–42.

Ives, Howard Colby. *Portals to Freedom.* Oxford: George Ronald, 1976.

Ives, Mabel Rice-Wray. "Grace Robarts Ober." *The Bahá'í World: A Biennial International Record, Volume VIII, 1938–1940,* comp. Prepared under the supervision of the National Spiritual Assembly of the Bahá'ís of the United States and Canada with the approval of Shoghi Effendi. Wilmette, IL: Bahá'í Publishing Trust, 1942, pp. 656–59.

Kempton, Honor. "Corinne Knight True," *The Bahá'í World: An International Record, Volume XIII, 1954-1963,* comp. Prepared under the supervision of The Universal House of Justice. Haifa: The Universal House of Justice, 1970, pp. 846–49.

Kinney, Pat. "Unity Feast Offers Taste of a Prejudice-Free World." February 10, 2000. http://bahai-library.com/newspapers/021000-2.html.

Lacroix-Hopson, Elaine. *'Abdu'l-Bahá in New York: The City of the Covenant.* New York: NewVistaDesign, 1999.

Lauchner, Aden J. "Albert C. Killius—Photographer of 'Abdu'l-Bahá," *World Order* (Spring 1999), pp. 42-43.

Maḥmúd-i-Zarqání, trans. Mohi Sobhani with Shirley Macias. *Maḥmúd's Diary: The Diary of Mírzá Maḥmúd-i-Zarqání*

Chronicling 'Abdu'l-Bahá's Journey to America. Oxford: George Ronald, 1998.

"Message to the Jews," *Star of the West* 3, no. 13 (4 November 1912), pp. 3–7, 10–11.

Metelmann, Velda Piff. *Lua Getsinger: Herald of the Covenant.* Oxford: George Ronald, 1997.

Morrison, Gayle. *To Move the World: Louis G. Gregory and the Advancement of Racial Unity in America.* Wilmette, IL: Bahá'í Publishing Trust, 1982.

Mortenson, Fred. "When a Soul Meets the Master." *Star of the West* 14, no. 12 (March 1924), pp. 365–67.

Nakhjavání, Violette. *A Tribute to Amatu'l-Bahá Rúḥíyyih Khánum.* Thornhill, Ontario: Bahá'í Canada Publications and Nepean, Ontario: Nine Pines Publishing, 2000.

National Spiritual Assembly of the Bahá'ís of the United States. Letter written to all Local Spiritual Assemblies and Registered Bahá'í Groups. September 23, 2008.

Ober, Elizabeth Kidder, Matthew W. Bullock, Beatrice Ashton, "Harlan Foster Ober: 1881-1962." *The Bahá'í World: An International Record, Volume XIII, 1954-1963,* comp. Prepared under the supervision of The Universal House of Justice. Haifa: The Universal House of Justice, 1970, pp. 866–71.

Ober, Harlan. "Louis G. Gregory," in *The Bahá'í World: A Biennial International Record, Volume XII, 1950-1954,* comp. Prepared under the supervision of the National Spiritual Assembly of the Bahá'ís of the United States and Canada with the approval of Shoghi Effendi. Wilmette, IL: Bahá'í Publishing Trust, 1956, pp. 668-70.

Office of Public Information, Letter to Anthony David, 1999. http:// bahai-library.com/file.php?file=uhj_website_photo_bahaullah.

Parsons, Agnes. *'Abdu'l-Bahá in America: Agnes Parsons' Diary*. Ed. Richard Hollinger. Los Angeles: Kalimat, 1996.

Ruhe-Schoen, Janet. *A Love Which Does Not Wait*. Riviera Beach, FL: Palabra,1998.

Rutstein, Nathan, *Corinne True: Faithful Handmaiden of Abdu'l-Bahá*. Oxford: George Ronald, 1987.

Stockman, Robert H. *Thornton Chase: The First American Bahá'í*. Wilmette, IL: Bahá'í Publishing Trust, 2001.

Taherzadeh, Adib. *The Revelation of Bahá'u'lláh, Volume 3: 'Akká, The Early Years, 1868–77*. Oxford: George Ronald, 1983.

_____. *The Revelation of Bahá'u'lláh, Volume 4: Mazra'ih and Bahjí, 1877–92*. Oxford: George Ronald, 1987.

Thompson, Juliet. *The Diary of Juliet Thompson*. Los Angeles: Kalimát, 1983.

van den Hoonaard, Will C. *The Origins of the Bahá'í Faith in Canada, 1898–1948*. Waterloo, Ontario: Wilfrid Laurier University, 1996.

Ward, Allan L. *239 Days: 'Abdu'l-Bahá's Journey in America*. Wilmette, IL: Bahá'í Publishing Trust, 1979.

Whitehead, O. Z. *Some Early Bahá'ís of the West*. Oxford: George Ronald, 1976.

_____. *Some Bahá'ís to Remember*. Oxford: George Ronald, 1983.

_____ and Marzieh Gail. "Majory," *World Order* (Summer 1973), pp. 44–48.

Whitmore, Bruce W. *The Dawning Place: The Building of the Temple.* Wilmette, IL: Bahá'í Publishing Trust, 1984.

Wilhelm, Roy. "Knock, and It Shall Be Opened Unto You," in *In His Presence: Visits to 'Abdu'l-Bahá, Memoirs of Roy Wilhelm, Stanwood Cobb, Genevieve L. Coy.* Los Angeles: Kalimát Press, 1989, pp. 3–22.

"William Sutherland Maxwell, 1874–1952." *The Bahá'í World: A Biennial International Record, Volume XII, 1950–1954,* comp. Prepared under the supervision of the National Spiritual Assembly of the Bahá'ís of the United States and Canada with the approval of Shoghi Effendi. Wilmette, IL: Bahá'í Publishing Trust, 1956, pp. 657–62.

Windust, Albert R. "Mrs. Esther Tobin: 1863-1944." *The Bahá'í World: A Biennial International Record, Vol. X, 1944-1946,* comp. Prepared under the supervision of the National Spiritual Assembly of the Bahá'ís of the United States and Canada with the approval of Shoghi Effendi. Wilmette, IL: Bahá'í Publishing Trust, 1949, pp. 543-44.

Bahá'í Reference

Momen, Wendi, ed. *A Basic Bahá'í Dictionary.* Oxford: George Ronald, 1989.

Smith, Peter. *A Concise Encyclopedia of the Bahá'í Faith.* Oxford: Oneworld, 2000.

Selected Social History Sources

"About the Hot Springs Vapor Caves." http://www.yampahspa. com/caves.html.

"About the NAACP: History." http://www.naacp.org/about/history/ index.htm.

Bausum, Ann. *With Courage and Cloth: Winning the Fight for Women's Right to Vote.* Washington, D.C.: National Geographic Society, 2004.

Bland, John. "William Sutherland Maxwell Biography." http://cac. mcgill.ca/maxwells/willbio2.htm.

Boyd, Lydia, and Lynn Pritcher. "Brief History of the U.S. Passenger Rail Industry." Duke University Libraries. http://library. duke.edu/digitalcollections/adaccess/rails-history.html.

"Called W. K. Lathrop a Liar: George Bradish's Fiery Speech at a Church Meeting," *The New York Times* (11 May 1893): n.p.

Clay, Pappy. "The War Between the Central Pacific Brakeman and the Iterant Hobos, During the Golden Spike Era," February 12, 1969. http://www.nps.gov/archive/gosp/research/pappy_clay2.html.

"The David Starr Jordan Prize." http://www.davidstarrjordan.org/ index.html.

Davis, Ronald L. F. "Creating Jim Crow: An In-Depth Essay." http://www.jimcrowhistory.org/history/creating2.htm.

Encyclopedia of San Francisco. "Jewish Community." Entry Author: Stephen Mark Dobbs. http://www.sfhistoryencyclopedia. com/articles/j/jews.html.

Falck, Susan. "Jim Crow Legislation Overview." http://www.jim-crowhistory.org/resources/lessonplans/hs_es_jim_crow_laws.htm.

The Forest History Society. "If Trees Could Talk: Fueling the Fires of Industrialization—The Railroad and the Tie." http://www.foresthistory.org/Education/Curriculum/Activity/activ3/act3rr.html.

Frost, Elizabeth and Kathryn Cullen-DuPont, *Women's Suffrage in America: An Eyewitness History.* New York: Facts on File, 1992.

"History of the Churches in Teaneck," http://www.teaneck.org/virtualvillage/churchhistory/churchhistory.htm.

"History of Stanford." http://www.stanford.edu/about/history.

"History of the Temple." http://www.emanuelsf.org/about_gi_history.htm.

"In Search of the American Hobo." http://xroads.viginia.edu/~MA01/white/hobo/ridingtherails.html.

Jane Addams Hull House Association. "Who We Serve." http://www.hullhouse.org/aboutus/whoweserve.html.

Jane Addams Peace Association. "About the Jane Addams Peace Association." http://home.igc.org/~japa/about_japa.html.

Kemp, Barbara, and Robert S. Harding. "Pullman Palace Car Company Collection, 1867–1979 #181." The Archives Center, National Museum of American History, March 1986. http://americanhistory.si.edu/archives/d8181.htm.

"The Life and Times of David Starr Jordan. http://www.davidstarrjordan.org/lifetimes.html.

Commander Lightoller. "Titanic," in *The Story of the* Titanic *as Told by Its Survivors*. Ed. Jack Winocour. New York: Dover, 1960.

Louden-Brown, Paul. "Titanic: Sinking the Myths." Published April 1, 2002. http://www.bbc.co.uk/history/british/britain_wwone/ titanic_01.shtml

Mast, Gerald. *A Short History of the Movies*, 4th ed. New York: Macmillan, 1986. The Montessori Foundation. "Dr. Montessori's Legacy." http://www.montessori.org/story.php?id=262

The Montessori Foundation. "The Montessori Way." http://www. montessori.org/story.php?id=261.

Murray, Irena. "The Architecture of E. & W. S. Maxwell: The Canadian Legacy, Introduction." http://cac.mcgill.ca/maxwells/ introtxt1.htm.

Murray, Irena. "The 'Old Craze of Buying Books': The Libraries of Edward and William Maxwell." http://cac.mcgill.ca/maxwells/introlib1.htm.

Notre-Dame Basilica of Montreal. "Did you know . . . ?" http:// www.basiliquenddm.org/en/basilica/did_you_know.aspx.

"Press Room: Media Information for the Historic Hotel Colorado." http://www.hotelcolorado.com/pressroom.html

"Recording History: The History of Recording Technology." http:// www.recording-history.org/HTML/dicta_tech1.php.

Robinson, David. *From Peep Show to Palace: The Birth of American Film*. New York: Columbia University Press, 1996.

Robinson, Harry G., III, and Hazel Ruth Edwards. "The Long Walk: The Placemaking Legacy of Howard University." http:// www.howard.edu/campustour/longwalk/.

"Spiritual Comforts Take Root," http://www.teaneck.org/virtualvillage/Religious/Spirit2.html.

"Stanford Facts: The Founding of Stanford." http://www.stanford.edu/about/facts/founding.html.

"Tactics and Techniques of the National Woman's Party Suffrage Campaign." http://lcweb2.loc.gov/ammem/collections/suffrage/nwp/tactics.pdf.

"The Triangle Factory Fire." http://www.ilr.cornell.edu/trianglefire/narrative1.html.

U.S. Centennial of Flight Commission. "The Beginnings of Commercial Transatlantic Services." http://www.centennialofflight.gov/essay/Commercial_Aviation/atlantic_route/Tran4.htm.

U.S. Centennial of Flight Commission. "The Vin Fiz—the First U.S. Transcontinental Flight." http://www.centennialofflight.gov/essay/Commercial_Aviation/atlantic_route/Tran4.htm.

The U.S. National Archives and Records Administration. "Teaching With Documents: Photographs of Lewis Hine: Documentation of Child Labor." http://www.archives.gov/education/lessons/hine-photos/.

"W&H MAIN YARDS: Hopping Freight Trains." http://www.spikesys.com/Trains/hoboing.html.

Wilson, Midge and Kathy Russell. *Divided Sisters: Bridging The Gap Between Black Women and White Women.* Anchor: 1996.

Wormser, Richard. *The Rise & Fall of Jim Crow: The African-American Struggle Against Discrimination, 1865-1954.* New York: Franklin Watts, 1999.

BIBLIOGRAPHY

Yates, Henry B. "The Lives of Edward and William S. Maxwell."
http://cac.mcgill.ca/maxwells/essay/01.htm.